EURIPIL

EURIPIDES TALKS

Edited by Alan Beale

Bristol Classical Press

First published in 2008 by
Bristol Classical Press
an imprint of
Gerald Duckworth & Co. Ltd.
90-93 Cowcross Street, London EC1M 6BF
Tel: 020 7490 7300
Fax: 020 7490 0080
info@duckworth-publishers.co.uk
www.ducknet.co.uk

A catalogue record for this book is available
from the British Library

ISBN 978 1 85399 712 9

Typeset by Ray Davies
Printed and bound in Great Britain by
MPG Books Ltd, Bodmin, Cornwall

Contents

Contents

Contributors

Chris Carey is Professor of Greek at University College London.

Sir Kenneth Dover is Chancellor of the University of St Andrews.

Jasper Griffin is Emeritus Professor of Greek at Balliol College, Oxford.

Alex Garvie is Emeritus Professor of Greek at the University of Glasgow.

Richard Janko is Gerald F. Else Collegiate Professor of Classical Studies, University of Michigan.

Richard Jenkyns is Professor of the Classical Tradition at Lady Margaret Hall, Oxford.

Jenny March is Associate Member of the Classics Centre, Corpus Christi College, Oxford.

Carmel McCallum-Barry lectures in the Department of Classics at University College, Cork.

Richard Rutherford is Tutor in Greek and Latin Literature at Christ Church, Oxford.

Richard Seaford is Professor of Greek at the University of Exeter.

Alan Sommerstein is Professor of Greek at the University of Nottingham.

Preface

Most of the talks which appear in this volume were delivered before performances by Actors of Dionysus (**aod**). Some are printed from texts supplied by the authors, others (such as Richard Seaford's talk) are transcribed from unscripted lectures. Therefore in tone and style these talks are more relaxed and informal than the usual academic work of the contributors. I have tried to maintain a sense of informality and immediacy in the editing. While a few contemporary references have been excised, little has been added beyond line references and an occasional footnote when mention has been made of other work. Line references are all to the Greek texts, although most translations do not follow the original, or indeed any consistent lineation. This is a constant problem for students of the plays in translation.

'To marry the practical with the academic'[1] was an ambition of **aod** from its inception, and the pre-performance talks which began in its second season helped achieve that aim and create a more informed and critical audience for the company. From its second issue **aod**'s journal *Dionysus* became the obvious place for these talks to be published. In 2001 they were replaced by small collections of specially-commissioned essays, the most recent being on *Bacchae* (2006). It is from these **aod** publications that the present selection has been made. I have tried to maintain a balanced representation of what is best in these introductory talks and essays, but with a bias towards those which maintain a focus on the plays rather than on the historical or mythical background or theatrical history. Inevitably, when introducing Greek drama to the general public and school audiences, there is much to say about the different culture and conditions in which these plays were first performed. I have tried to give some help with the mythical background by adding a brief guide to the mythology for each play, which I hope will put the minor mythological details into context.

It has been a privilege to be associated with **aod**, who have now

---

[1] David Stuttard, *JACT Review*, 2nd series, no. 24, p. 12.

completed fifteen successful years bringing Greek drama to a wider audience than any other contemporary company. It is a measure of their success that distinguished scholars have generously given their time and expertise to further the company's aims. I would like to thank Tamsin Shasha, Artistic Director of **aod**, and David Stuttard, the Founder of **aod**, for all the help and advice they have given during the slow germination of this book. Thanks too to Deborah Blake who has been a patient and helpful guide throughout. To Central Newcastle High School I am grateful for a month of study leave. But my principal thanks go to the contributors for permission to publish their work in its current form.

Alan Beale

Introduction

The City Dionysia, at which Euripides' plays were first performed in the fifth century BC, was a festival in honour of Dionysus celebrated over five days at the end of March. It was not a festival solely for dramatic competitions. For example, it started with a great procession leading to the precinct of Dionysus where sacrifices were made. But the drama was the most significant part of the celebrations. We have no equivalent to a festival where a large audience (12,000-14,000 is a popular estimate) watched in the open air a series of four plays by each of the three playwrights in the competition for tragedy. That is at least twelve plays in three days – without taking the comedies into account.

Written for a large open-air theatre for performance by an all-male cast of three actors wearing masks and changing roles, these plays offer a huge challenge to a modern company. And what can you do with a chorus of 15 which plays a role in the drama and also sings and dances between episodes (roughly our scenes)? Given the finance and time, it can be done – as was triumphantly demonstrated by the National Theatre's *Oresteia* (1981). **aod**, on the other hand, have taken tragedy on the road with a small company of male and female actors. Sets and props have to be portable and easily assembled, costumes mostly easy to change and lighting flexible enough for different conditions. Their gruelling schedule on tour has taken them across most of the country, often playing to audiences with little opportunity to see Greek tragedy on stage. In these circumstances 'authenticity' is not an option.

But even if **aod** aimed at authenticity, sufficient historical and archaeological evidence does not exist for us to be able to replicate confidently the theatrical conditions in Athens at the time of first performance. No costumes, no masks survive. Even the representations of these we have on vase paintings rarely belong to the fifth century. Those that do, show elaborately decorated costumes with tight-fitting long sleeves, at least for the main actors, allowing freedom of movement for the arms. Representations of

1

the Chorus show costumes less restrictive around the legs, presumably for dancing. Masks seem strikingly realistic, although
one must take note of the tendency for painters to depict the
actors 'melting' into their parts and showing the same facial
features as their masks. For props and scenery there is even less
clarity. While a number of plays contain descriptions of the
surroundings, and we are told that Sophocles invented scene
painting, there is no hard archaeological evidence. The depiction
of a rocky archway on a number of vases seems to show a
theatrical prop, but we cannot be sure whether such an image is
an accurate representation of what appeared (or didn't) on stage.
Even the theatres themselves don't offer a clear picture. While
the theatre at Epidauros offers the most attractive model, other
theatres are very different or have been altered significantly in
later periods. The Theatre of Dionysus at Athens, the very home
of Attic tragedy, was the venue for less exalted entertainment at
times in the Roman period, and the Roman remains visible today
conceal only tantalising vestiges of the fifth-century theatre,
which are hard to interpret with any certainty.

It is with good reason then that **aod** have adapted the plays
for the wide variety of venues in which they have performed, from
school halls to large theatres. From relatively 'straight' translations and a traditional acting style, the company moved further
from 'authenticity', first by embracing the methods of physical
theatre, especially in their production of *Bacchae* in 2000, and
secondly by writing adaptations, the first of which was *Medea* in
2001. Their most recent production, *Bacchic*, is the most extreme
form of adaptation they have attempted, creating an entirely new
play, set in the modern world and performed by one actor using
only a rope for a set. Despite the departure from producing the
original tragedies, **aod** remains true to its purpose, only now they
seek by indirections to find direction out. Actors of Dionysus took
their name from the Greek guilds of itinerant actors which
formed in the third century BC. They have metamorphosed into
aod as they have developed their distinctive style.

The essays presented here are firmly aimed at the original
tragedies. Of extant tragedies, all but one have a mythological
setting and, as far as we can tell, the playwrights were free to
adapt myths to their purpose, sometimes with minor adjust-
ments to the established version(s), sometimes, it seems, with
quite drastic adaptation (if Euripides was the first to have Medea

kill her own children). The short guides to mythological detail which precede the talks lay out the myths as told in each play, drawing together scattered references into a sequential narrative. It has been often said that members of the Greek audience knew the stories in advance. Perhaps that is true, although doubt has been cast on this assumption. It is how the playwright uses the myth that is significant, and to understand how cleverly Euripides does this one must go to the plays ... and the talks.

BACCHAE

Bacchae, 2003. **aod** perform in the ancient theatre at Ephesus, on their first
Swan Hellenic cruise. Tamsin Shasha as Dionysus; chorus played by
Marianna Maniatakis, Kirsten Shaw, Kate Gabriel and Jenny Ayres.
Photo: daveashtonphotography.com

The circumstances of the writing and first performance of *Bacchae* are unknown. The play came to light after Euripides died in Macedonia in 406 BC and was produced in Athens some time later.

aod tours in 2000 and 2003; adapted as *Bacchic*, 2007-8.

Guide to mythological detail

Bacchae, also called maenads, are the female followers of Dionysus, and the play takes its name from the Chorus of his female devotees who have accompanied him from Asia to Thebes where he means to establish his rites in the face of opposition from members of his own family.

Foundation myth and the 'sown men'

Cadmus, son of Agenor, left Sidon in search of his sister Europa. Directed by Apollo to follow a cow with white marks and to found a city where it lay down to rest, Cadmus founded Thebes (170-2). There he had to kill the resident dragon. Advised by Athena, Cadmus sowed the dragon's teeth from which there shot up armed warriors. Cadmus flung a stone into their midst, making them turn on each other. From the ensuing battle there were five survivors (the 'sown men') of whom Echion was one. Cadmus married Harmonia, daughter of Ares (1357), and with her had four daughters, Autonoe, Ino, Agave and Semele. He gave Agave in marriage to Echion and they had a son, Pentheus, whose heredity is frequently referred to in the play and used to characterise him by the Chorus (537ff.).

The birth of Dionysus

When Zeus fell in love with Semele, another of Cadmus' daughters, and made her pregnant, his jealous wife Hera persuaded the innocent girl to bind Zeus by oath to appear to her in all his majesty. As a result she was consumed by his thunderbolts, but since the unborn child Dionysus was immortal he was rescued and spent the rest of his gestation sewn up in Zeus' thigh. Semele's sisters slandered her by claiming that Zeus had killed her because she attributed her pregnancy to him in order to hide her transgression with some mortal lover (26-31). This calumny Dionysus is determined to punish. Besides, Agave's son Pentheus has now become ruler of Thebes and he too refuses to accept Dionysus as a god. Dionysus' first action has been to drive the women of Thebes in madness from their homes and onto the slopes of Mount Cithaeron outside the city.

Cadmus' future

When Dionysus appears at the end of the play he makes a strange prediction about Cadmus' future. Firstly, he and Harmonia will be turned into snakes. Secondly, they will ride in an ox-cart at the head of a barbarian army and destroy many cities. Finally, they will go to the land of the blessed. (1330ff.).

Bacchae: a sexy sect and the death of a statesman

Jasper Griffin

Of all Greek tragedies this, with the single possible exception of *Antigone*, is the most resonant for modern people. It seems to present us with a scenario with which we are comfortable, a story pattern familiar to us in *bien pensant* contemporary cinema and television drama: a black Puritan (and for the modern *bien pensant* person all Puritans are of the black, repressed, life-hating kind) has his carefully hidden lusts unmasked; then he is destroyed by his repressed desires and contradictions.

But when a work composed several thousand years ago, for a very different society, seems so modern, then we need to be especially on our guard. It is then that we over-simplify, make mistakes, and fail to distinguish things which present a superficial appearance of familiarity. It is in order to make that point that I include in my title the word 'sect'. It is a current term of shock and horror; sects destroy families, are denounced in the newspapers, and deny the tenets of society. They are much more alarming than Puritans. We are not, really, much worried nowadays about Puritans, who are on the defensive, in retreat or in full flight. But that does not mean that there are not still groups by which society really is alarmed: groups which challenge and shock the community.

Let us begin by looking at the mythical pattern of the play in a simpler and less problematic form. We find it, very conveniently, in a poem composed probably a hundred years or so before the *Bacchae*. It is a hymn, traditionally ascribed to Homer, in honour of the god Dionysus. It tells how one day the god, in appearance a well dressed and rather soft young man, long haired and seemingly effeminate, was strolling by the shore of the sea. A ship came by, full of pirates; they immediately decided to kidnap this helpless figure and hold him to ransom, or sell him as a slave. But once they had him on board, things began to go wrong. The captive, imperturbable, smiled at them with his dark eyes, and the ropes with which they tied him fell off; down the mast tumbled vines, heavy with grapes; ivy, the other sacred plant of the god, sprouted in the rigging; the air was filled with the sweet smell of wine. Then wild beasts appeared, a lion, a shaggy bear: they caught the wicked captain and killed him, while the other sailors leapt overboard in terror and were changed into dolphins. Only the helmsman, who had recognised the god and urged the others to abandon their blasphemous attempt, was spared, and he was sent off to be a missionary and servant of Dionysus. Moral: worship Dionysus!

This charming and uncomplex poem offers what is clearly the same story as the *Bacchae*. The god seems helpless, he is exotic, soft, girlish, no match for macho men, but when violence is used against him, it recoils on the user. The god retains the imperturbable calm of one who knows his own superiority, and his attackers go mad and destroy themselves or are destroyed. The god gives the appearance of being a victim. He is specifically oriental in appearance. He embodies that combination, so baffling to the ordinary male: long haired, musical, soft, at every point the opposite of the manly man, he is nevertheless inexplicably more attractive to women than the regular guys with short back and sides and no effeminate nonsense about music. We observe another thing, too, about this Dionysiac figure. He is for choice not at home in the city, with its settled pieties and regular rules, but somewhere else, out in the wild, away from the world of schools and political parties, somewhere closer to nature. And nature can be kindly and alluring, but also inhuman and terrifying.

You will not have to reflect long before you see the parallel with the figure, hated and adored, of the male rock star, surrounded by his female adorers. They may try to tear off his clothes, a transparent substitute for the *sparagmos*, the act of tearing apart the animal victim which in a sense is the god; they may kiss the bared torso, a transparent substitute for the desire to devour him – as the maenads first tore their victim to pieces and then feasted on its raw flesh. In the play Pentheus, when he has been induced to don the Dionysiac dress and so to identify himself with the god and also with his victim, will be torn to pieces; his mother, in her altered state of consciousness, carrying her son's head, will ask the Chorus if they want to taste the flesh of her catch.

Common to the hymn and to the tragedy is the god's lack of

resistance, his unshakeable and increasingly sinister calm, as he smiles with dark eyes; and in both, the offence against him is followed by the transformation of nature itself. That can be kindly: as the pirate mast puts out the fruit of the vine, the pious maenads can carry fire on their heads, suckle serpents, and draw from the earth milk and wine. It can also be hostile and terrifying. Violence and imprisonment prove futile. Animal forms appear; in the play Dionysus is said to have the forms of lion, of serpent, and when he is in his power, Pentheus sees him as a bull. The victim goes crazy and acquiesces in his own destruction.

This story pattern recurs repeatedly; Homer tells us, for instance, in *Iliad* 6.130-40, of the brutal Lycurgus, who tried to manhandle the god, and who came memorably to grief. It is *the* myth of Dionysus. The god appears, he is slighted and attacked, and he destroys his persecutors. In its basic form it is morally and emotionally simple and satisfying. We shed no tears for the enemies of the god. Good enough for the rat – he got what was coming to him! Two hundred years after the *Bacchae* the poet Theocritus still tells it in that straightforward way (*Idyll* 26). But in our play, the *Bacchae*, the old pious tale is made into something much more complex.

Let us ask a simple question: What is Dionysus god of? One of his titles is *Dendrites*, God of Trees. He is associated with the sap which springs up in plants and animals alike, and which makes certain animals formidable – the snake, the lion, and the bull: as we hear at lines 1017-19 – Manifest yourself *as bull or many-headed serpent or blazing lion*. And Pentheus does see him as a bull, horned, 920. The bull is a formidable creature, when seen from close quarters, heavy with a sense of destiny and power. The maenads see Pentheus as an animal, 1108; a calf, 1185; a lion, 1215, 1278. That is in line with what we find in the real cult of the god in many places in Greece.

In the words of the intellectual Tiresias, he is god also of 'moist food', and above all of wine (278ff.). Why wine especially? Because it is what most powerfully embodies and releases the life force within us, which abolishes distinctions, which frees us from the rational vision of the *polis*, from the usual rules and restraints, and from the governance of the all too male spirit of political order and discipline. We feel oneness with the universal ground of being. We could be friends with wild animals; we could lift mountains (as Pentheus feels that he could, 945ff.). It is not primarily sexual, though Pentheus, trapped in his rules and his refusals, thinks it is. And it frees us from dignity – maenadism is not dignified, and the early scene with Cadmus and Tiresias underlines that, as the old men feebly dance and are scorned by the young and virile king. But for him there will be worse. Trying to maintain his dignity, Pentheus loses it disastrously, and consents to parade through the city in female dress, a mark for universal derision.

Dionysus is a god of the outside, an incomer into the city community. He disregards and disrupts the *polis*, and he sends the women out of it and out of their clearly defined Greek female role. An effeminate Easterner defeats the king; women leave their children and rout soldiers. Civilised life demands periodic release, reversal, even explosion: especially the restricting life of women. To deny this means big trouble. That is one thing which we see here.

But the god denies more than just 'politics'. Boundaries are crossed on a much bigger scale, contradictories reconciled: the Chorus sing of the *charis*, the grace of eating raw flesh (139), an act normally taboo; women carry and suckle serpents, from which they would normally recoil in horror. They carry fire. The earth itself becomes (again?) a nursing mother. When the maenads set upon the armed men and defeated them, 'the whole mountain joined in the Bacchic dance; so did the wild beasts, and there was nothing that was not moved by the onrush' (726-7). When Pentheus is to be grabbed and torn to pieces, fire comes from heaven, a supernatural voice is heard, and women perform extraordinary feats of physical strength.

Dionysus shows his unhuman nature. But this has two sides. They are immediately juxtaposed, early in the play, when the Chorus sing of 'hunting the blood of a goat, the grace of raw meat, over the mountains, with Bacchus our leader, *euoi*: the ground runs with milk and wine and honey' (135ff.). The maenads are persecuted; when spied upon, they are 'a miracle to see of good order' (693); they sing a beautiful prayer for peace and the calm of pastoral escape (403ff.); yet they are also the terrible creatures who, though female, rout the army of the *polis* and tear Pentheus to pieces. Both sides are essential. Dionysus, we hear, is (in the same line!) both 'most terrible' and also 'most gentle': *deinotatos* and *epiotatos* (861).

What are we to make of this vision and this religion? Initially, we think that Pentheus has some right on his side. The life of the community is being catastrophically disrupted. The scene with the aged Cadmus and Tiresias preparing themselves to dance on the hills is very close to comedy; and it presents two types of those who hang on the fringes of religion. Tiresias is the intellectual, the guru, with his high flown theoretical account of the new faith; Cadmus is the time-server, who thinks all this is good for the prestige of the family, and who first claims 'I shall never weary of dancing to the god', and then expects to be driven to the site in a chariot ('Surely we aren't going to walk?' 191). But soon we see Pentheus as a bully and a thug, shouting and persecuting. He tries to hunt the maenads, and he sets out to hurt old Tiresias (346ff.). Also he is obsessed with sexual fantasies: shocking things, he knows, are going on! That obsession will be the key to his undoing. Dionysus deftly uses it to destroy him. 'So you want to see what is offensive to you?' asks the disguised god. 'Yes, I do ...' (815ff.). So Pentheus ends up, a doomed voyeur, dressed as a woman, in the hope of seeing what he loves to hate.

And so our perspective changes again. Increasingly we see Pentheus as a victim; the hunter becomes the quarry (228, 352, 434, 451, 866ff.), and we hear more and more of the net, the hunting hounds, the 'trophy' which is Pentheus' head (848, 977, 1108, 1141-2, 1171). But our moral attitude changes, too. When we sympathised with his victims and disliked the prurient persecutor, we did not realise how far his disaster was to go: that we should witness the Chorus exulting as his mother in crazy triumph carried her son's severed head. And then we are forced to confront the god's treatment of the rest of the family, which is pitiless and horrible. Readers of Euripides may compare the end of *Medea*. There, too, we felt sympathy for Medea, ill treated by the ignoble Jason; but we had not realised that by the end of the play we should see her murdering her own children. In both plays our sympathy has in the end no easy place to go, and the poet denies us the simple pleasure, which we naturally want, of having our wishes granted: the nice characters rewarded, and the nasty ones punished.

So at the end the inhuman side of Dionysus comes uppermost, in a way that makes complex the simplicity of the ancient myth pattern. The man who fought against the god and was rightly smashed is made human and complex. He is given a family: a mother, a grandfather, people who mourn his terrible end. The

13

broken humans plead for mercy; the god is merciless. They plead in vain. Euripides' Dionysus embodies both the qualities of an impersonal force of nature, and also the touchiness and vindictiveness of an all too human person (we can compare the goddess Aphrodite in Euripides' *Hippolytus*). He and his religion are at once beautiful and horrible. A simple cult story has achieved the complexity, and the stature, of tragedy.

The paradox of the *Bacchae*

Alex Garvie

Bacchae is a play of paradoxes – the paradox of an oriental god who brings his religion from Asia to Greece, and yet was born to Zeus and Semele in Thebes; the paradox of a new religious cult which Tiresias will claim to be as old as time itself; the paradox of a choral entrance-song whose theme is the cult of an oriental god, yet which takes the form of a traditional Greek hymn; the paradox of Dionysus as a god whose cult proclaims blessedness only for those initiated into his Mysteries, but who is also the god of the ordinary man, and who demands worship from everybody, irrespective of their gender or their age; the paradox of an ecstatic religion which requires moderation and good sense in its practitioners. This essay will concentrate on the most striking paradox of all. The god who throughout the play promises joy will at the end produce only suffering and horror.

We meet Dionysus first in the prologue. He explains to us how he has travelled from Asia to introduce his new religion to Thebes. But his aunts deny his divinity and have been driven mad, with all the women, into the mountains, where they are sitting peacefully under the silver-fir trees, while Pentheus, the young king of Thebes, is resisting the new religion. Dionysus therefore plans to manifest himself to Pentheus and to the whole of Thebes, before moving on to some other land. The tone is unemotional and factual. All the emphasis is on the manifestation of Dionysus' divinity, and there is not a word about punishment for Pentheus, little to rouse either our sympathy for the god or our disapproval of his plan. Before he departs he explains that he has disguised himself as a human votary of himself. Only at the end of the play will he appear again in his divine form.

If the tone of the prologue is unemotional, that of the Chorus' entrance-song is quite the reverse. This is indeed one of the most exciting entrance-songs in the whole of Greek tragedy. The irruption of the oriental god into Greece is represented for us by the

15

Chorus of his oriental followers, who have travelled with him from Asia, as they irrupt into the theatre, dancing wildly and singing in emotional rhythms, to the accompaniment of drums. The keynote of the song is the blessedness of the initiates, and the exciting joy of going to the mountain to dance in ecstasy. Note the recurring ritual cry, 'to the mountain, to the mountain'. If this is what Dionysiac worship means, how can anyone be against it? At this early stage we hardly notice the single brief reference to the more violent aspect of the cult, the joy of hunting a goat and eating it raw (139). And, if we have some faint misgivings about the escapism that it involves (the women on the mountain have abandoned their housework!), they are entirely overshadowed by the overall mood of joy. We are certainly not yet encouraged to think about what will come back from the mountain at the end of the play. The Chorus will play a vital part in this tragedy, as it guides our emotional reaction. Joy will be the theme of most of its songs, but, as was shown in a study published forty years ago,[1] there will be a progressive degradation in its understanding of that joy.

We have noted the dramatic change in mood between prologue and entrance-song. Equally striking is the reversal of mood between entrance-song and the following episode. The aged prophet Tiresias arrives on stage to summon the equally aged Cadmus, the grandfather of Pentheus, so that they can go off to the mountain to worship. Clad in Dionysiac fawn-skins, carrying Dionysiac wands (*thyrsoi*), and wearing ivy-garlands on their heads, they look forward to taking part in the wild dancing on the mountain, claiming that they alone in Thebes have good sense. Cadmus calls Tiresias 'wise', but what is the relationship between rational wisdom and the demands of this emotional religion? Does one not have to be 'mad' to join in Dionysiac dancing? They are joyful because they have forgotten their old age, and feel that they can dance all night and day. The irrational is not confined to any one age-group, but there is something a little ridiculous about the spectacle, and the mood descends almost into bathos when Cadmus, despite his claim to be rejuvenated, asks pathetically if they cannot go to the mountain on a carriage (191).

So far we have seen Dionysus through our own eyes and

[1] J. de Romilly, 'Le Thème du bonheur dans les Bacchantes', *Revue des études grecques* 76 (1963), 361-80.

16

through the eyes of his followers. But now we are to see him through the eyes of Pentheus, his principal antagonist. Pentheus in his opening speech makes clear his reasons for opposing this new religion: it is merely a pretext for luring women into the mountains to indulge in illicit sexual unions (223-5). He mocks the effeminate appearance of the supposed votary (235-6). Like a typical stage-tyrant he thinks that violence is the solution to all problems, and plans to hunt down and imprison the women on the mountain (228-32). Tiresias and Cadmus do their best to persuade Pentheus to change his mind, Tiresias by means of a number of sophistic arguments, which no doubt justify Cadmus' description of him as intellectually 'wise' (179), but which leave out entirely the excitement of the Chorus' entrance-song. Joy has now become the pleasure of drinking wine, which helps one to sleep and to forget one's troubles (280-3). Dionysus is the god of wine, so there is nothing false about this argument. But Dionysus is so much more besides, and, after the excitement of the en-trance-song, Tiresias' defence of the new religion is clearly inadequate. When he accuses Pentheus of being mad (326), he forgets that madness is an essential part of Dionysiac religion. Cadmus' justification for worshipping the god is even less satis-factory: even if Dionysus is not a god, it will be good for the honour of the family to pretend that he is (333-6). He accuses Pentheus of having no good sense (332), the quality on which the two old men have prided themselves. It is hardly surprising that by the end of the episode Pentheus remains unconvinced, and departs with orders to his men to arrest the votary and bring him back to face execution by stoning.

The choral song which follows deals again with Dionysiac joy, but gone now is all the excitement of the entrance-song. The Chorus takes its cue from the arguments of Tiresias, and pre-sents Dionysus in conventional terms as essentially the god of wine and of peaceful convivial parties (380-5). The ode is full of the commonplaces of Greek thought. Moderation and wisdom are praised, and the wisdom is that of the common man (427-31). Again we feel that there is something lacking. At the beginning of the next episode we are suddenly reminded of what the ode omitted. Enter a servant with the 'votary' under arrest. The servant describes how Pentheus' men 'hunted down' their prey, and here now is the 'animal' which they have caught (434-6). The metaphor foreshadows the way in which Dionysus, at this stage

17

of the play the prey, will later turn into the hunter of Pentheus. So begins the first of three confrontations between the god and Pentheus. It ends with Pentheus apparently in control, as the votary is led off to prison in the palace-stables. But already we have a sense that the god is merely playing with him.

In the next choral ode Dionysus is again seen as a god of wine. The Chorus cannot understand why Thebes rejects the joy which he brings, and calls on him, not yet to punish, nor to take vengeance on, Pentheus, but merely to put a stop to his outrageous behaviour (*hybris*, 555). The song is interrupted by the voice offstage of Dionysus, who is miraculously released from his prison, and who now appears on stage to describe how he sat quietly as Pentheus rushed around in a futile attempt to bind a bull, which he mistook for the votary (618-22). Given that Dionysus has already been described in the entrance-song of the Chorus as the 'bull-horned god' (100), it is a pardonable error. Enter Pentheus, totally bewildered by the escape of his prisoner. He is closely followed by a herdsman, who, in the first of two formal messenger-speeches in this play, has come to report the behaviour of the women on the mountain. At first all is peaceful and idyllic, but the mood soon changes. The herdsman and shepherds set out to 'hunt' (719) the women, as a pleasant sport. But it is the women who hunt the hunters. They tear the cattle in pieces with their bare hands, and the fragments are hanging from the trees dripping with blood. For the first time in the play the keynote is violence, but as yet the principal victims are animals, not human beings. The women go on to raid the neighbouring villages, and succeed in wounding men. But this detail is passed over lightly, and the women finally return to the peace of the mountain. Violence and peace are juxtaposed, and it is left to the Messenger to draw a wholly inadequate moral: this is a powerful god, who has given us the vine which stops our pain – without wine there is no pleasure for men (773-4).

Pentheus, failing totally to appreciate the power of his antagonist, resolves to lead his army against the women on the mountain. But Dionysus, in the second confrontation between the two, offers instead to take him, with no army, to spy on the women. First, however, he must put on female clothes, so that he may remain undetected. Pentheus at first recoils, but it is clear that he really wants to see the women engaged in their immoral activities, and, although he pretends, as he leaves the stage, that he has not yet made his decision (845-6), we know that it is in fact already taken, and that he is already lost. After his departure Dionysus has the last word. It only remains for him to make his enemy mad. Pentheus is heading for a hunter's net. For the first time in the play we are explicitly told that he is to be punished, and that death will be his punishment (847). But first he must become a laughing-stock for all the Thebans, as he walks through the city dressed in female clothes. The last line of Dionysus' speech (861) sums up the paradox of this religion: 'a god most terrible, but most gentle to mankind'.

The choral song that follows begins with a sense of movement and excitement that we have not heard from the Chorus since its entrance-song. It looks forward to its joy, when, like a fawn that has escaped from the hunting-nets, it will be fully free to worship the god. But the sense of excitement does not last. Soon we return to the platitudes of Greek thought, and the joy at the end of the ode has deteriorated into that of momentary pleasures: 'that man whose life is happy day by day, him I call blessed' (910-11). The third confrontation between Dionysus and Pentheus is the most unpleasant. Pentheus, now completely under the god's control, totally destroyed from a psychological point of view, and giggling as he fusses about his hair and the fall of his woman's dress, sets off happily with Dionysus to see the sexual activities of the women on the mountain. It is not a pretty sight. His last words are 'I am getting what I deserve' (970). If till now we were not sure whether or not to sympathise with Pentheus, there can no longer be any doubt.

The following choral ode is the most exciting since the entrance-song, and, unlike the previous ode, there is no diminution of that excitement at the end. The Chorus call on the swift hunting-dogs of Madness to go to the mountain, to incite the women to take vengeance on the man who has gone to the mountain to seek them out. 'I enjoy hunting', they say (1005). Pentheus, the hunter, is to become the victim of the hunt. The manifestation of justice (compare the theme of manifestation in the prologue) is now unequivocally identified with the killing of Pentheus. Finally the Chorus call on Dionysus to appear in his bestial form, as a bull or a serpent or a lion, and with smiling face to cast a noose round his victim (1017-23). The violence which was merely hinted at in the entrance-song is now uppermost in our minds.

19

This is the cue for the appearance of the second messenger, who comes to announce Pentheus' death. The chorus-leader's first, triumphant, reaction dismays the Messenger. 'What are you saying? Do you really rejoice at my master's misfortunes, lady? ... It is not right to rejoice at the evil things that have been done' (1032-3, 1039-40). In a full-scale formal messenger-speech he describes for us these evil things. The climax comes when the mad Agave, Pentheus' mother, ignores her, now sane, son's appeal for pity, and, together with the other women, tears him limb from limb. She is now on her way back from the mountain, carrying Pentheus' head in triumph on her *thyrsos*, 'priding herself on her hunt', in her delusion thinking that it is the head of a lion. This, then, is what Dionysiac joy has become, the joy of a mother who has killed her son. The Messenger ends with a moral that is as banal as that which concluded the earlier messenger-speech: 'Moderation and respect for the things of the gods are best; I think that this is also the wisest possession for mortals who practise it' (1150-2). The gulf between the platitude and the horror of what the Messenger has reported is very striking.

In a brief lyric passage the Chorus maintains the triumphant tone. And then Agave enters, carrying her grisly burden from the mountain, to join the Chorus in a highly emotional lyric dialogue. The themes of joy and hunting continue to be interwoven, but there is a telling moment when even the Chorus, till now completely sympathetic to Dionysus and hostile to Pentheus, expresses revulsion at Agave's invitation to join her in eating the raw flesh of the 'lion' (1184). Cadmus reappears, carrying the pieces of Pentheus' body which he has gathered on the mountain. At first his grief contrasts with Agave's continuing joy. But Cadmus begins the process of enlightening her. At first she tries to evade the truth, feeling perhaps instinctively that she can remain happy only as long as she is still mad. But eventually she is forced to accept it, and the joy is gone for ever: 'Alas, what do I see? What is this that I am carrying in my hands? ... Unhappy me, I see a most painful thing!' (1280-2). And the cause of her suffering is clear to her: 'Dionysus has destroyed us, as now I understand.' Cadmus sums it up: 'Wretched am I, miserable are you [Pentheus], pitiable your mother, miserable your relations.'

At the end of the play there is no joy for anyone. Even the Chorus has found it too much to bear. It is the punishment of Cadmus which seems most unfair, as even the chorus-leader acknowledges: 'your grandson has the punishment which he deserved, but it is painful for you' (1327-8). He who set off for the mountain to worship Dionysus, not indeed for the best of motives, suffers as much as anyone else. We may suppose that this is merely a case of the innocent suffering along with the guilty, but that is not exactly how Euripides presents it. The manuscripts break off after the chorus-leader's expression of sympathy, and, when they resume, Dionysus is on stage, no longer in disguise, in the middle of a speech, prophesying that Cadmus is to be transformed into a snake and driven into exile. 'If you [plural – he includes Cadmus in the whole family] had known how to show good sense (or 'moderation'), when you did not want to, you would have been happy, having acquired the son of Zeus [i.e. Dionysus himself] as ally' (1341-3). Cadmus might, we feel, have replied that he had indeed done his best to behave in the manner that Dionysus now recommends, and that what he has learnt is that moderation and good sense are the last things that are required in the worshipper of this god. Instead, he concedes that 'we have done you wrong', and complains only that Dionysus has gone too far in his vengeance. 'Gods', he says, 'should not be like mortals in their tempers' (1348). The trouble is that they are. Scholars used to argue about whether in this play Euripides is arguing in favour of Dionysiac religion, or, on the contrary, that the god does not deserve to be worshipped, if he exists at all. Most critics now recognise that to put the question in these terms is mistaken. The power of the irrational, which Dionysus represents, does undoubtedly exist, and there is no point in saying that one is either against or in favour of it.

Is there any hope at all at the end of the play? We might like to suppose that Dionysus drives mad only those who reject his divinity, and that if we worship him properly he will bring us only joy. But the play gives us little guidance as to what his proper worship would be. Cadmus, who did his best, suffers with the rest, and even the Chorus has its moment of revulsion. The comfort that Cadmus and Agave offer each other is only temporary; for, as the play ends, they depart to their separate exile. Richard Seaford, the most recent editor of the play, in an interesting interpretation,[2] sees the suffering as a necessary prelude

---

[2] Richard Seaford, *Euripides, Bacchae: with an introduction, translation and commentary* (Warminster: Aris and Phillips, 1996), 48-52.

to the foundation of Dionysus' civic and communal cult in Thebes. The royal family had to destroy itself and be driven out before the city could begin to practise it. Pentheus is thus to be seen as a kind of scapegoat whose destruction benefits the whole city. It is true that in the prologue Dionysus announces his intention of manifesting himself to all the people of Thebes, and we might expect the effect on the community to play some part at the end of the play. But, as we have it, nothing at all is said about it. This may be why the loss of part of the final scene in the manuscripts is so disastrous; for it may be there that this optimistic idea was developed. All that we can safely say, however, is that in the play as it stands there is no optimism at all at the end. And, even if the interpretation of the lacuna is correct, it is surely the horror that predominates. Somehow the despair seems all the darker because of the recurring theme of joy that has preceded it. The play was written in monarchic Macedonia, but presented in democratic Athens, in the theatre of Dionysus, as part of the god's festival. He is the patron god of tragedy as well as comedy. His concern is with suffering as well as laughter. He may bring joy, but the potential for that joy to turn to tragedy is always present.

What ought the Thebans to have done?

Alan H. Sommerstein

Something goes terribly wrong in *Bacchae*. The god Dionysus, son of the Theban princess Semele, has returned to Thebes to establish his cult there. Every spectator watching the play at the City Dionysia knows that this cult, like Dionysus' gift of wine, can bring great pleasure and great release of mental tension. And yet its arrival in Thebes produces catastrophe. Semele's nephew Pentheus, the king of Thebes, is torn in pieces by his mother Agave, her sisters Ino and Autonoe, and the other women of Thebes; Agave returns to Thebes in triumph, believing she has killed a lion, and displaying Pentheus' head on the end of her ritual rod (*thyrsos*); and finally the entire family, including Agave's aged father Cadmus, are expelled from the city. Why has this happened?

In one sense, Dionysus himself answers this question right at the beginning. Semele, made pregnant by Zeus, had perished through the guile of Zeus's ever-jealous consort Hera. The story (told somewhat allusively in *Bacchae*) is that Hera, in disguise, persuaded Semele to ask Zeus to visit her in his full divine splendour; Zeus, having promised Semele to do whatever she wished, could not refuse her request, and the lightning-fire of his presence destroyed her. Zeus snatched her unborn infant from the flames and sewed him up in his own thigh, eventually to be 'born' a second time.

Cadmus turned Semele's house and tomb into a shrine (6-12). Her sisters Agave, Ino and Autonoe took a very different view (26-31). They claimed that Semele had really been pregnant by a mortal lover, and at her father's suggestion had covered her shame by pretending Zeus was the father of her baby, and that Zeus had destroyed her to punish this lie. Because of this slander, the three sisters, with all the other women of Thebes, have been 'driven in madness from their homes', and made to wear Dionysus' sacred garb and perform his rituals (32-8).

That, however, need not have had catastrophic results. If

Thebes, as Dionysus puts it (39-40), 'learn[s] ... that it is uniniti-
ated in my bacchic cult', and adopts it officially, Dionysus will
doubtless let the women go home (cf. 804-7). But will Thebes do
that? Not if Pentheus has his way. He 'fights against the gods',
says Dionysus, 'or at least against me, debars me from libations,
and does not mention me in his prayers' (45-6); he may try to
bring the women home by force – in which case Dionysus will 'join
with the maenads as their general' (52) with unstated, but evidently fatal, results for Pentheus.

Dionysus' indictment of Pentheus may at first sight seem a
little unjust. Pentheus was abroad when Dionysus came to Thebes (215), and has had no way of knowing that he even exists,
much less that he demands universal worship. What is more, it
is perfectly reasonable that he should believe Semele's infant had
perished (since that is what normally happens when a pregnant
woman suffers a violent death, and no one in Greece knows of any
evidence to the contrary) and perfectly reasonable that he should
believe the baby's father was not Zeus (for Zeus would not have
destroyed his own offspring). But whatever sympathy we may
initially have for him is dissipated with extraordinary rapidity as
we get to know him better. Dionysus' condemnation is quite
unjustified in terms of what Pentheus had done previously; but
what Pentheus does subsequently shows, at the very least, that
he was riding for a fall of some sort.

Pentheus starts putting himself in the wrong almost from the
moment he appears. He has imprisoned numerous free-born women
in chains (226-32) on the basis of unsubstantiated rumour ('I hear'
216, 'they say' 233). If he catches their priest (who is really Dionysus
in disguise) he will execute him by stoning (356) or by decapitation
(241) – a punishment utterly abhorrent to Greeks – and there is no
indication that there will be any trial. He tells his own grandfather
that he is making a ridiculous fool of himself (250-2, 344-5). He
accuses the prophet Tiresias of being complicit in the introduction
of the new cult in the hope of increasing his professional income
(255-7) – and we know that when someone accuses Tiresias of
corruption it is always a bad sign (ask Oedipus, or Creon in *Antigone*); later he orders the physical destruction of Tiresias' seat of
augury (346-51), thus putting himself in the wrong with Apollo as
well as Dionysus. No wonder Tiresias ends the scene (367-9) by
hoping that Pentheus, whose name means 'man of grief', may not
bring grief to Cadmus and his family.

So far, as we have seen, Pentheus has spoken and acted entirely on the basis of rumour – some of which will prove completely false (notably the allegation that the women's bacchic rites are a cover for sexual debauchery). Now he begins to receive authentic information, which makes it obvious that a god is at work. The guard who has arrested the supposed priest reports that the imprisoned women have been miraculously liberated, their feet being unchained, and the prison doors opened, by no mortal hand (443-8): Pentheus' response, incredibly, is to order the guards to let go of the priest's arms, 'because now he is in the net, he is not speedy enough to escape me' (451-2). It is as if he had not heard what had just been said to him – not the last instance of such selective deafness or blindness. And after an interview in which contempt of the new cult is strangely mingled with curiosity (cf. 471-80), he has the 'priest' locked up in the palace stables, and gratuitously adds that his Asian followers will be seized as slaves (511-14).

There follows another miracle, or series of miracles, of which this time Pentheus is an eyewitness. A mighty voice is heard; the palace shakes; the sacred fire on Semele's tomb suddenly flares up; and presently the 'priest' walks calmly out of the palace, his prison having been demolished. Pentheus meanwhile has been kept busy tying up a bull (618-21), fighting the fire, and trying to kill a phantom (629-31). Surely by now he must have some suspicion that he is up against something too powerful for him? Not in the least: his next order is to close all the city's gates (653) as if this were a routine jailbreak.

The final proof that Pentheus' whole approach is both false and dangerous comes immediately afterwards, as a herdsman arrives with news from Mount Cithaeron. He has seen the bacchants on the mountain, and they are as orderly as a military garrison. They are divided into three companies, each under a commander (680-2), they rise promptly at reveille (689-94) and adjust their uniforms carefully (695-8), they perform their rituals at fixed times (723-4), and sexuality and drunkenness are nowhere to be detected. On the other hand, the impossible and the miraculous seem to be matters of routine: the women use live snakes as belts (698), suckle fawns and wolf-cubs (699-702), and by a stroke or a touch make the ground flow with milk, honey, water and wine (704-11). All utterly amazing, and utterly unthreatening – except of course that society will collapse if the women aren't restored to sanity, and to Thebes, fairly soon. This, though, cannot be done by force, as the rest of the herdsman's narrative makes clear. When he and his friends, encouraged by a know-all from the city (717-21), try to capture the women, they immediately run amok, tear cattle in pieces, raid two villages and put the armed inhabitants to flight; and loads do not burden them, fire does not burn them, weapons do not wound them. How will Pentheus respond to this?

He responds in his accustomed manner. He has by now witnessed, or been credibly informed of, fifteen or twenty manifest miracles. And as ever, he neither accepts nor denies their reality; he just ignores them. He orders an immediate military expedition against the bacchants (780-5), vowing to 'stir up a great deal of women's blood' on Mount Cithaeron (796-7) – oblivious, it seems, to the fact, of which we have recently been repeatedly reminded (682, 689, 720, 728), that one of these women is his own mother. It is perhaps significant that he refers to them as his 'slaves' (803), as if he were the king of Persia – doubly ironic, this, considering how he prides himself on his Greekness (483, 779) in contrast to barbarians like the Lydian 'priest' and his followers. We now expect the threatened military expedition (cf. 52) to be launched, and Dionysus to take command of his maenad army as promised. What happens is rather different.

For at this moment Dionysus shows that he is, after all, a god of justice. Pentheus has shown himself a tyrant with no respect for man or god, ready to insult his grandfather, imprison or kill his mother, chop off heads on mere suspicion, and treat free people like slaves, wilfully blind and deaf to the plainest evidence that a superhuman agency is at work – and yet Dionysus offers him a way out. 'I will bring the women here', he says, 'without the use of arms' (804). Thebes can be restored to normality without any blood being shed. Of course, there is a price: the definitive establishment of Dionysiac cult at Thebes (807-8). But why on earth not? On all the available evidence, the cult brings pleasure and, unless provoked, no pain. But Pentheus will have none of it: 'Bring me my armour out here. And you, stop talking.' (809)

The disguised god doesn't stop talking, and Pentheus never gets his armour; in fact, the next time we see him he will be dressed as a woman, and the time after that he will be a set of detached body parts.

Pentheus' approach to the Dionysiac phenomenon has been a disastrous failure, and this naturally leads us to ask what alternative approach, if any, could have been successful. The play actually offers us a considerable range of options, before it narrows its focus to show us the consequences of the one chosen by Pentheus.

The first of these options is presented by the Chorus of Lydian bacchants in their opening song (*parodos*). One part of this song narrates the birth(s) and infancy of Dionysus; other parts give a detailed and evocative picture of his ecstatic worship, first in the streets (64-87), then in the mountains (135-69). The song is full of 'barbarian' elements: the women are Asian, they wear the weird garb of bacchic ritual, carry and doubtless beat drums; there are repeated references to Lydia, Phrygia, even Syria, all of which to the Greek mind were places that slaves came from. The mountain ritual consists of running, leaping, falling, dancing, singing, shouting, with drums, pipes and torches, and its focus and object is to hunt down goats, tear them in pieces and eat their raw flesh (139). It may well be doubted how anyone could think it wise to introduce such practices as this into a society that wished to be sane and safe. In particular, a crucial psychological prerequisite, apparently, is what the Chorus call 'communalising the soul' (75-6): abandoning individuality, merging one's personality in the swarm. Such an experience can be extremely uplifting and pleasurable. It can also, however, be extremely dangerous: 'herd instinct', 'crowd hysteria', 'mob violence', are all designations of what can happen if this process gets out of hand. The Greek *polis* is a place where law rules and where the individual citizen is responsible for his actions. At the very least, even if one accepts that a degree of uninhibited release may be beneficial, it must be kept within some kind of boundaries. There is no sign that this Chorus is willing to accept anything of the kind. They claim authority over the streets and houses and their inhabitants (68-70); they become animalised, wearing fawnskins and galloping like fillies (137-8, 164-9); they tear animals apart as if they owned them, not caring that goats might have a goatherd. If this is what Thebes and Pentheus are being offered, one can well understand if they feel they have to reject it.

Next we see two Thebans, Tiresias and Cadmus, both aged men. They may not be able to gallop like fillies or tear goats in pieces, but they do believe it is their duty to join in the worship of Dionysus. They have, though, two very different approaches to the cult.

The fate of Cadmus in the play may well seem unjust. Early in the prologue Dionysus praises Cadmus for creating a shrine to Semele (10-11), and we learn also that he, unlike his daughters, had always publicly maintained that Semele's lover had been none other than Zeus. On learning that Semele's son has returned to Thebes as a god, Cadmus is eager to do him honour. That Cadmus is in the end bereaved of his treasured grandson is of course not inconsistent with this: the punishment of the guilty inevitably has side-effects on their innocent kin. But Cadmus also receives from Dionysus a specific punishment of his own: exile from Thebes to a barbarian land, and transformation into a snake (1330-4, 1354-60). It is true that he will eventually go to the Isles of the Blest (1337-8), but overall his fate is undoubtedly meant as a punishment, as Dionysus makes clear in words that are addressed to Cadmus as well as his daughters:

> If you had known to be sensible, when you refused to be, you would now be happy, with the son of Zeus for your ally. ... You have understood us too late; you did not know us when you should have done. ... I was a god, and you insulted me. (1341-7)

And Cadmus admits the charge (1344, 1346, 1377-8), even while pleading for mercy. What is he admitting being guilty of? If the play offers an explanation at all (and surely it ought to), it must come in the scene in which Cadmus and Tiresias are confronted by Pentheus. It may not matter much that Cadmus tells Pentheus that 'even if, as you claim, this god does not exist, you should pretend he does' for the honour of Semele and the family (333-6); taken by itself, that might be just Cadmus desperately trying to get through to Pentheus with an argument that might possibly appeal to him. But Cadmus had spoken like that to Tiresias too:

> I have come prepared, wearing this sacred attire of the god; for since he is my daughter's son, it is right that he should be magnified and glorified to the best of our ability. (180-3)

Admittedly Cadmus, as the first mortal ever to have a god for a grandchild, is in a unique position with no precedent to guide

28

him, but his language strongly suggests that he is magnifying and glorifying Dionysus only because Dionysus is his grandson – doing, in fact, precisely what he later recommends Pentheus to do, and 'telling a fine lie' in the family's interest. His attitude also changes the significance of what we heard in the prologue: the insistence that Semele's lover had been divine, the creation of a shrine to her, now look like the contrivances of a head of family determined to put a positive spin on what might have been a very shaming episode. To say the least, we cannot be sure he actually believes that Dionysus is a god.

Now it is true that Greek religion, generally speaking, was a matter of practice rather than of belief. The gods, on the whole, didn't mind what mortals thought about them, so long as they received their dues in the form of prayer and especially sacrifice. But as the trial of Socrates would soon show, belief couldn't be ignored, because it could have an effect on practice. If the belief spreads that the gods do not really exist, sooner or later the community will decide that it can use its resources better than by sending them up in smoke to these non-existent gods – and if by any chance the gods do in fact exist, such a decision could have unfortunate consequences. And Dionysus, in particular, can only be truly worshipped by those who throw their whole being into the act of worship – and one can hardly be doing that if one is thinking of Dionysus as a family asset. It is therefore appropriate that whereas the Chorus of Asian devotees condemns Pentheus (263-5) and praises Tiresias (328-9), they say nothing at all about Cadmus.

Tiresias, in tragedy, is nearly always right, and the audience may well look to him for some words of pious wisdom in an attempt to set Pentheus on a more prudent path. They may perhaps be disappointed. Tiresias speaks less like a prophet than like a sophist. He rationalises everything; all the mystery and the ecstasy disappear. Dionysus is the inventor of (or perhaps is) wine, which is good for drowning sorrows, inducing sleep, and pouring in libations (280-4). He was never sewn up in Zeus' thigh; that story was created through the confusion of two similar-sounding words (292-7). He also has (in reality rather minor) connections with prophecy and war (298-305). And while Dionysus will not compel women to be chaste, a woman who is truly chaste by nature will not change her nature under his influence (314-17) (which, for an overwhelmingly male audience that was

29

not disposed to think particularly highly of women's moral capacity, would beg a very big question). All this is all very well, but it has little to do with the kind of ecstatic worship that we have heard partly described, partly enacted by the Chorus in their opening lyric. It is an attempt to tame Dionysus and make him into a reasonable god that reasonable, educated late fifth-century Athenians can rationally worship. If that is the kind of god he wants to be, he would never have come to Thebes accompanied by these outlandish barbarian women.

Or so we probably think, until the scene ends and the outlandish barbarian women sing their second ode. And to our surprise we find that all the wild ecstasies have vanished, to be replaced by the not exactly sober, but at any rate bounded and socialised pleasures of that civilised, urban(e) institution, the symposium (376-85). The Chorus commend 'a life of quietness and good sense' (389-90) and warn against the danger of 'not thinking mortal thoughts' and of 'chasing great things' instead of making the best of what one can get (395-9). They pray to be taken to Cyprus or Pieria (402-16), the lands of Aphrodite and of the Muses. The connection between Dionysus and the Muses would be obvious to every Athenian spectator; and Aphrodite, as the Herdsman will remind us (773-4), is (in the right context) an essential part of the good life. In the final stanza Dionysus' association with 'the painless delight of wine' is re-emphasised, as is his democratic nature: he offers his gifts 'equally to the prosperous and the inferior' (421-2). More than once the Chorus express a rejection of what may be called intellectualism (*to sophon*, 395); true intelligence (*sophia*) is something different – it is accepting the human condition and the opinions and practices of 'the masses of ordinary people' (430). This distinction between two contrasting connotations of *sophia* – being clever enough to know what's good for one, and being too clever for one's own good – runs right through the play.

Is this the answer we have been seeking? It seems surprisingly banal and naïve, and resolutely oblivious to the tragic aspects of human existence. Accept life's pleasures – song, dance, food, drink, sex, sleep, and good company (the listing is Kenneth Dover's – in another, though still Dionysiac, context – and all of them figure in the choral ode we have been looking at); don't try to rationalise them into conformity with some high-flown philosophical schema; respect popular traditions, especially religious ones; that is true wisdom, and will bring happiness. Naïve or not, this view does seem to be endorsed by all the Theban commoners we see in the play. The guard who arrested the disguised god was reluctant to do so and told his prisoner as much (441-2), and he tells Pentheus 'this man ... is full of miracles' (449-50). The herdsman, though fearful of the king's anger (670-1), urges him to accept the new god, not least because 'they say ... he gave mortals the vine which puts a stop to grief; and if there is no more wine, there is no more Aphrodite, nor any other human pleasure' (771-4). And the Messenger who reports Pentheus' death concludes that 'to know one's place (*sophronein*) and revere the divine is best, and I think it is also wisest' (1150-1).

There is, after all, no contradiction in believing that life has both its tragedies, many of them unavoidable, and its pleasures, and that since total renunciation of the pleasures will not help one escape the tragedies, it is foolish not to accept them (within reason, of course). If Pentheus has rejected normal pleasures (and one certainly doubts if he'd make a good companion for a symposium), it seems only to have led him to seek perverted ones: his way of showing affection for his grandfather had been to ask whom Cadmus wanted him to punish (1310-12, 1318-22), and he is lured to his death by being offered the chance to spy on the maenads' alleged sexual orgies. And his evidence-proof hatred and contempt for Dionysus and all he stands for leads to an appalling catastrophe that was entirely avoidable.

It remains true that though Pentheus and Cadmus, Agave and Ino and Autonoe, have all deserved to suffer, they all suffer far more than they deserve, or than anyone deserves – and that is the note on which the play ends. It may well be, as Richard Seaford supposes,[1] that Dionysus' speech as *deus ex machina* (most of which has been lost from the only manuscript) included instructions for establishing an organised cult of Dionysus at Thebes; but the Thebans who will benefit from that cult are not on stage. Those who are present are Cadmus, the lonely old man facing a future he loathes; Agave, the mother who has killed her son; and that son's dismembered body, over whose torn limbs, one by one, Agave, in another lost passage, had lovingly lamented. As often in Euripides, human love seems the only consolation in a cruel

---

[1] Richard Seaford, *Euripides, Bacchae: with an introduction, translation and commentary* (Warminster: Aris and Phillips, 1996), on lines 1329-30.

world: father and daughter part with an embrace (1363-7), and
Agave will share her exile with her sisters (1381-2). They themselves may have made the world crueller than it need have been,
but we can pity them nevertheless – as even the Chorus do
(1327-8).

And we can go a little beyond pity. In the play's last genuine
words, Agave says:

> May I go where
> foul Cithaeron shall never see me again
> nor I set eyes on Cithaeron,
> and where no *thyrsos* is dedicated, to remind me!
> Let them be the concern of other bacchants! (1383-7)

Just as the savage zeal of Pentheus was counter-productive, so
too, at least in one respect, has been the zealous savagery of his
cousin Dionysus. It has benefited nobody, at least in Thebes
(since Dionysus could have destroyed Pentheus, or rendered him
harmless, in many less atrocious ways), and it has irrevocably
alienated this sister of Semele. It is entirely understandable that
Agave should thus loathe and shun that which caused her ruin.
She cannot be expected to reflect – but we should – that so many
things in this world have caused the ruin of someone at some time
that we cannot possibly shun them all. We have seen in this play
that Dionysus is a risky, destabilising god; but deliberately,
obsessively to avoid all risk and instability is itself risky and
destabilising. And deliberately, obsessively to avoid pleasure as
such merely ensures that life will be all pain – as if there wasn't
enough of that anyway.

MEDEA

Medea, 1996. Tamsin Shasha as Medea.
Photo: Adrian Gatie

Performed at the City Dionysia in the spring of 431 BC, *Medea* was the first play of a trilogy (plus satyr play) which was only awarded third prize.

The **aod** production of 1996 was followed by a tour of David Stuttard's adaptation in 2001.

Guide to mythological detail

Medea's past

Her homeland was Colchis, a distant, barbarian city on the eastern shore of the Black Sea where her father Aeetes, son of Helios, was king. It was to this land that Jason came on the *Argo* to take away the Golden Fleece (1-6), but in order to achieve his goal, he had to perform two impossible tasks set by Aeetes. Medea fell in love with him (8), but in her account (496-7) he had to make appeals and vows to win her support. It was only because of her help that he was able to yoke her father's fire-breathing bulls and sow the dragon's teeth (476-9). She also claims that she killed the serpent which guarded the fleece (480-2). After such betrayal of her father and native land (31-3, 483), Medea secured her escape with Jason and the fleece after killing her brother (167) at his hearth (1334), a sacred place which adds to the horror of the crime. (Although the motive isn't stated, it may have been to delay her father's pursuit, as in the version with murder and dismemberment at sea.)

When they reached Jason's home, Iolcus, Medea engineered the murder of Jason's uncle Pelias at the hands of his own daughters (9-10, 486-7, 504-5) and for this crime she and Jason were driven into exile. Now in Corinth, Jason has decided to marry the daughter of Creon, the king (17-19), in order to give his family the security that only comes with wealth and position. Jason and Medea have two young sons (47-8).

Euripides Talks

Medea's present

In the prologue we hear from the Nurse of the devastating impact of Jason's betrayal: Medea shouts, will not eat, lies collapsed in agony and is in tears (20-7). Then in her anxiety the Nurse fears that Medea may harm the children (36-7). At that moment the children appear with the Tutor who brings news of her impending exile. The Nurse's fears for their safety are made explicit (90-5). Then we hear the savage cries of Medea in her grief, issuing threats against Jason and his whole house including their children (112-14), and later Jason and his new bride (163-5).

After her confrontation with Creon, in which she secures one day to prepare for exile (340ff.), her resolve is to kill Jason, his new bride and Creon (375). After Aegeus has promised her refuge in Athens, falls the bombshell: Creon and his daughter remain targets for murder, but now it is not Jason, but her children she will kill (792-3).

Medea's future

In the final scene, Medea is transformed. Raised aloft on the chariot of her grandfather Helios, she returns to her strange roots and now almost assumes the role of a goddess. She predicts Jason's future: an unheroic end lies in store for him, struck on the head by a fragment of his ship, the *Argo* (1386-7). Medea, her children dead at her feet, will not accord Jason the satisfaction of giving them burial, but will bury them herself in the precinct of Hera Acraea and establish rites to be performed by the Corinthians to atone for their murder (1378-83). Then she will go to Athens and live with Aegeus (1384-5). When she gets to Athens, what lies in store? On the rest of her life Euripides is silent. But the Athenians knew stories closer to home: that she would have a son by Aegeus, would attempt to kill Theseus, Aegeus' son by Aethra daughter of Pittheus. They have received a hint in 679-87 where Aegeus reveals he is on his way to Troezen to consult Pittheus about the oracle he received in response to his enquiry about having children.

Euripides and a mother's grief

Jenny March

Of all the three great tragedians of the fifth century BC, it was Euripides who had the most interest in mother/child relationships in his plays – and not just interest, but an almost uncanny insight into the kinds of feelings a mother might have. Sophocles barely refers to mothers and children. In Aeschylus we have Clytemnestra's grief over her dead daughter Iphigeneia in the *Agamemnon*. But in Euripides, mothers, and their love for their children and their grief at their deaths, are a major element in play after play after play.

Now, I want to begin by looking briefly at the *Medea* that we shall be seeing tonight, then to put it in the context of Euripides' other works, and to talk about mothers and children in a few others of his plays. Finally, we shall come back to *Medea* in more detail.

The setting of *Medea* is Corinth. Here Medea and Jason fled after Medea had murdered old king Pelias of Iolcus. Some years have passed. Medea has had two sons by Jason. But, as the Nurse says in the Prologue, 'Now all is hostility, and love has turned sick' because now Jason has deserted Medea and has married the daughter of Creon, king of Corinth. The play centres on Medea's revenge. Savage with jealousy and rage she at first plans to murder all three of the people who have wronged her – Jason, Creon and the new bride. But her final revenge is more horrible: she kills Creon and the new bride, yes. But she also kills the two sons she has had by Jason, and she leaves Jason himself *alive* to suffer forever the terrible results of having betrayed her.

Now, Euripides was a great innovator in his plays (never believe it if you hear that when the Greeks went to the theatre, they knew just what would happen in a play because they knew their myths. The tragedians made lots of changes when they came to put those myths on the stage). And what is new here is Medea's murder of the children. You can find the details in the Introduction to Page's edition of *Medea*, but briefly: in earlier

37

versions of the legend, before Euripides, the children died, yes, but for other reasons. In one version, Medea unintentionally killed them while trying to make them immortal (remember, she was a kind of witch and had magic powers). In another version, the Corinthians killed them in revenge after Medea had killed Creon. But Euripides made Medea herself *choose* to murder them as part – and in fact the most hurtful part – of her revenge against Jason.

So here, as the climax of the play, a mother voluntarily kills her own children; and Euripides shows us the torment in her mind, the mixture of rage and grief, that she feels as she does so. So let's look at some other plays of Euripides, at mothers and children, and specifically at children's deaths, to put this play into context.

In some plays, children are killed, but not by their mother; by an outside enemy. As an example of this, we have the *Trojan Women*. This play is set in the aftermath of the Trojan War. Troy has been conquered, the Trojan men are dead, and here are the Trojan women about to be carried off as concubines and slaves by the Greeks. One of these is Andromache, the wife of the great Trojan warrior Hector. She has a little son called Astyanax, and the Greeks, urged on by Odysseus, decide that Astyanax must be killed, for if he is left alive he may, when he becomes a man, take vengeance for his father's death and for the destruction of his city. The news that he must die – that he will be flung from the walls of Troy – is brought to Andromache, and she grieves for her little son's fate as she holds him in her arms:

Child, you cry. Do you know your death is coming?
Why do your little hands clutch and cling to my gown,
like a young bird come to nestle under my wings?
And Hector will not come. He will not come,
great spear in hand, back from the earth to save you,
nor will his kinsmen, nor all the power of Troy.
A deathly fall from the walls will break your neck
and choke your breath, with none to pity you.
Little one, here in my arms, your mother's darling,
how sweet the smell of your skin! All for nothing
this breast nursed you, you in your baby shawls,
all for nothing now my toil, my weary labour ...

Euripides, *Trojan Women* 749-60

38

Medea

'All for nothing': this is what mothers of dead children so often say in these plays. It will, ironically, be what Medea herself says[1] and the Chorus will echo just before she kills her sons – 'All for nothing' (*Medea* 1029-31 and 1261-2).

Andromache herself can do nothing to protect her son, because next in the play she is carried off to be the slave of Neoptolemus (he's the son of Achilles, the very man who killed her beloved Hector). And Astyanax is killed, flung from the walls of Troy. His body is brought onstage, carried on his father's great shield to his grandmother, Hecuba, Hector's mother. And she in turn laments his fate, mourning over his broken body:

> Poor little head, how cruelly your father's walls,
> the towers built by Apollo, have rent your curls
> that once your mother so often tended and kissed,
> and now your blood grins out from the broken bones ...
> What could a poet write of you on your grave?
> 'This child the Greeks once killed because they feared him.'
> Words to bring everlasting shame on Greece.
> Now you have lost all that your father had,
> but one thing you shall keep, this shield of bronze
> in which to sleep ...
>
> Euripides, *Trojan Women* 1173-93

And Astyanax is dressed and carried out for burial, with Hector's shield for his coffin.

So in *Trojan Women* the child is killed by an outside enemy, while the mother – and the grandmother – grieve. Other plays where children are killed, leaving the mother to grieve, are the *Iphigeneia at Aulis*, where Iphigeneia is sacrificed to raise winds for Troy; and the *Hecuba*, where Hecuba has to stand by while her daughter Polyxena is sacrificed by the Greeks to appease the ghost of Achilles, and then finds that her son Polydorus – the last son she had left alive – has been killed by Polymestor, the very man to whom she had sent the boy for safety. Polymestor killed him for the sake of the gold that he had. And this, coming on top of Polyxena's death, changes Hecuba from a figure of helpless grief and despair to one of raging, avenging fury. With the complicity of Agamemnon, Polymestor is summoned to the Greek

---

[1] *Trojan Women* 760 is almost identical to *Medea* 1030.

camp. When he arrives, together with his two little sons, Hecuba lures him into her tent with the promise of more gold. Here her serving women are waiting. Polymestor is quite at ease, thinking that he has nothing to fear from a crowd of mere women, but they overpower him with their sheer numbers. They stab his sons to death with their own weapons, then blind Polymestor himself by gouging out his eyes with their brooches. And so Polydorus is avenged – and that's what this mother did as a reaction to her son being murdered. In this play, as in the *Medea*, a mother turns to murder to get her revenge, killing the children of her enemy – though in the *Medea* they are her own children too.

Now I would like to look at another kind of play that Euripides was particularly fascinated with, a type of plot that was one of his favourites, where a son is separated from his mother in infancy and grows up quite apart from her. Then many years later mother and child meet again, but don't recognise each other; and for some good reason the mother tries to kill the son, or the son the mother, or both, until in the nick of time they realise the truth and are joyfully reunited with one another. As an example of this kind of play, we have Euripides' *Ion*. Here Ion is the son of the Athenian princess Creusa, born to her after she was raped by Apollo. Afraid of her parents' anger, she sorrowfully abandoned her baby in a cave under the Acropolis, but on Apollo's instructions the boy was carried to his temple at Delphi by the god Hermes. Here he was found and taken in by Apollo's priestess, who brought him up in the god's service while all the time he believed himself to be an orphan. Creusa meanwhile believed her son to be dead, carried off by wild beasts from the cave in which she left him – she went back to look for him, and he was gone. She married a man called Xuthus. For many years the couple had no children. Now in the play they come to Delphi to consult the oracle about their childlessness, which is a source of pain to both of them, but particularly to Creusa, who is torn apart with longing for a child and with sorrow for her lost son, believed dead.

Xuthus consults the oracle and is told that the first person he meets on leaving the temple will be his son. He meets Ion, who at first believes that this stranger joyfully greeting him as his son is mad; but eventually matters are straightened out and they assume that Ion must be Xuthus' illegitimate son, the result of some youthful indiscretion. Both agree that they must tell the news to Creusa with great tact, but before they can do so, Creusa learns from her servants that Xuthus is intending to bring into the family a bastard son. So she plans to murder Ion. She gives a phial of poison to a faithful servant, who secretly puts it into Ion's cup at a feast. But as Ion is about to drink, he hears an ill-omened word spoken and says that all cups should be refilled with fresh wine. He pours his wine on the ground, and when a dove drinks it and dies in agony he realises that this drink must have been poisoned. He learns from the servant the truth about Creusa's intention to murder him. He goes to find her, and is about to kill her in punishment when the priestess intervenes, bringing out the cradle in which long years ago Ion had been found as a baby. Creusa recognises it at once, and to prove it she describes one by one the little items she left in the cradle with her child: a piece of weaving, a golden necklace, an olive wreath. One by one the priestess holds them up for Ion to see, and mother and son are finally reunited with great joy: she has her son back again, and he has at last the mother he never knew and always missed. Xuthus remains content in the belief that he is Ion's father, and the family return in great happiness to Athens. This is called a tragedy, but it's one of the ones with a really joyous ending.

So there the mother almost kills her son, then is almost killed by him, before their moving recognition takes place. Other examples of this kind of plot are the *Alexandros* (a lost play, known only from fragments), where Hecuba, after exposing Paris at birth, came across him years later and tried to kill him, not knowing he was her son, but found out the truth just in time; and the *Cresphontes* (also known only from fragments), with a similar plot, where Merope tried to kill her unknown son Cresphontes with an axe, though he was somehow recognised by a servant just in time. This scene with the axe probably happened actually on stage, which must have been very dramatic. Plutarch mentions it, saying 'What a stir Merope makes in the theatre, sending the audience rigid with fright.'

So in all those three plays, the mother tries to kill her son, but recognises him in the nick of time. But in the *Bacchae* – this is getting closer to the *Medea* – a mother actually kills her son, and only recognises him after he is dead. In this play, the god Dionysus comes in disguise to Thebes, intending to prove to the Thebans that he is a god. Thebes is being ruled by Pentheus, a very young man, who refuses to worship the new god, Dionysus. At the start of the play, Dionysus has driven all the women of the city mad, and they've run away into the mountains. They are up on Mount Cithaeron, worshipping Dionysus, raving as maenads. Among them is Pentheus' mother, Agave.

Dionysus avenges himself on Pentheus by driving him mad too, and taking him up on to Mount Cithaeron disguised as a maenad. Here Pentheus has to face the other maenads, who are led by his mother, Agave. She thinks in her madness that he is a mountain lion, and Pentheus, himself restored to sanity and a terrible knowledge of what is going to happen, tears the headdress from his hair that she might recognise him. 'Mother', he cries, 'it is I, your own son, Pentheus. Don't kill your son!' But Agave is blind to the truth, and she and the other maenads tear Pentheus to pieces. She then triumphantly carries his head back to Thebes, still believing it to be that of a mountain lion. There her father Cadmus brings her gently back to sanity, to recognise that she is holding in her arms the head of her own son, whom she herself has killed. To my mind, that recognition in the *Bacchae* – a mother recognising her own dead son – is the most moving and dramatic and effective recognition in the whole of Greek tragedy.

So – we've thought about plays where children were killed by outsiders; plays where a mother unwittingly tries to kill a child, and he is saved in the nick of time; a play where a mother actually kills her child, though she is mad and doesn't mean to. And so now to the *Medea*, where Medea in her right mind chooses to kill her sons. But in killing them, she kills a part of herself.

She formulates her idea of killing Jason's sons after her scene with old king Aegeus of Athens. He calls at Corinth on his way back from the Delphic oracle, where he was looking for advice on his childlessness (like Creusa and Xuthus in the *Ion*). This reminds Medea of how important having sons is to a man. So when she is alone again, she says that Jason's new bride will die, as she planned earlier, but she will also kill her own and Jason's sons. This will hurt Jason most (817) since he will be left alive to endure a sad and lonely old age. This was one of the worst fates to a Greek, not to have children to tend you when old (cf. 1032-5).

Medea makes her plans. She will pretend to forgive Jason, to be reconciled with him, to have a complete change of heart. 'I shall speak soft words to him', she says (776). Then, when he is taken in by her and no longer suspicious of her motives, she will send gifts to the princess – a poisoned robe and crown. Well, everything goes according to plan. Jason praises Medea for her change of heart. He greets his sons and prays for their future lives, speaking with pride of their growing into fine young men (914-21). At this Medea weakens, and Jason asks her why she's crying, and she answers, 'When you prayed that they might live, sorrow overcame me in case this might not happen' (930-1). The audience can appreciate the irony of this, aware that Medea knows the children have no chance of growing up at all, because she means to kill them. But despite her regrets, she still persuades Jason to let her send gifts off to the princess – and off the boys go with them. So there is no going back now, because the princess is bound to die from the poisoned robe and the crown. Everything has gone according to plan.

Except that at the last minute Medea says that she really can't bring herself to kill her sons, and in a long monologue she debates whether she will do it – no she won't, yes she will, no she won't, yes she will. This really must have been a high spot of the play, because the audience wouldn't have known what her final decision would be – remember, the deliberate murder of the children by Medea was Euripides' innovation, so the audience would have been on the edge of their seats. This, in brief, is how the monologue goes: Medea begins by grieving that now she must be parted from her sons: she must go into exile, while they – though they don't know it – are going to die. All for nothing (remember Andromache saying this over Astyanax in the *Trojan Women*) she bore them and brought them up, and they will never now look after her when she is old. 'What shall I do?' she cries (1042). And then (I paraphrase), 'No, I can't do it. Goodbye to my plans' (1044). But then the opposite: 'What am I saying? Do I want to be laughed at by my enemies? I have to do it! How could I even entertain such soft thoughts!' (1049-52). Then again: 'But no, my passion, don't do it. Spare their lives. Only if they live will they bring me happiness' (1056-8). Again, back to firmness: 'And yet I have no choice. Now the princess is dying by her gifts. I must kill my sons before my enemies do so. I have to travel the cruellest of roads, and send these children on a crueller road still' (1067-8).

And so she does in the end decide to kill the children, and now the audience know it will happen, but for a long time they can't have been sure which way it will go. It's a long monologue, and a gripping one, and I'm looking forward to seeing it performed tonight.

Now Medea's tormented monologue, trying to decide what to do, shows, I think, brilliant insight by Euripides. We have the two sides of Medea's nature battling against each other – the rejected wife fighting with the loving mother – her all-consuming passion for revenge in conflict with the clear knowledge that by killing her children she will hurt herself the most – her passionate emotional side at war with her rational, logical intelligence. In a sense she kills her children because of the uniting of these two aspects of her nature: it is her passionate desire for revenge carried to its logical conclusion – what will hurt Jason the most. But without this insight into Medea's nature, without this genuine conflict, without the grief she feels as a mother, the play would not be tragedy but simply melodrama. And at the end of the play we see the results of Medea's fateful tragic choice, when the angry, rejected wife wins out over the mother who genuinely loves her sons.

First, though, there is one more very significant speech by Medea (1236-50). The princess and Creon are dead, killed by the poisoned gifts. Now Medea must finish off her plan and kill her sons. And these are her very last words before she goes indoors to carry out her dreadful deed, where we see very clearly her resignation and grief at her choice of action: 'Friends [she says to the Chorus], my course of action is clear: as quickly as possible to kill the children and then leave this land, not delay and give my children over to be killed by another and less loving hand. They are bound to die in any case, and since they must, then I shall kill them, I who bore them. Come, my heart, steel yourself. Why do I hesitate before this fearful yet necessary evil? Come, wretched hand, take the sword, take it; go forward to the point where life turns into grief. No cowardice, no memories of your children, how dear they were, how your body gave them birth. For one short day forget your children – and then weep. For though you kill them, yet they were dear ...'

That to me is another brilliant insight by Euripides, a supreme understanding of a mother's reactions. The children must die now, because the Corinthians will want revenge for their murdered king and princess. And the mother's reaction is: 'they must die, so let it be me who kills them; me, the mother who bore them. Let them at least die by a loving hand.' So in the end, Medea kills them out of love. And in killing them, she kills a part of herself.

For those are Medea's last words spoken on the human plane

of the stage. The next time we see her, after the children's dying screams have been heard offstage, is high up on the dragon chariot of the Sun, on her way to safety in Athens. She appears where the gods normally appear, and she seems to speak with a god's tone, giving judgement and prophesying the future. She gloats over the poor, human, grieving Jason down below. And in fact she seems to have been transformed, become herself something more than human, as if by killing her children she has lost all her humanity. In the Prologue to the play, the Nurse likened her in her grief to a rock or a wave of the sea (28-9). Now she has destroyed the human part of her by her child-murder, and has truly become quite as inhuman as a rock or a wave of the sea. Earlier she wept over her children, but she has now become so changed, so hardened, that we doubt if she will ever weep again. At the end of the play, the wife of Jason may stand in triumph in her dragon chariot, gloating over the man who betrayed her – but Medea the mother is dead.

Euripides' *Medea* and the manipulation of sympathy

Richard Janko

Euripides is a master of the unexpected, and especially of the unexpected turn of events and our reaction to them. When the *Medea* opens, there is no doubt as to where our sympathies lie. Our reactions to Greek tragedy are guided by those of the characters in the play and the dramatist is very careful to guide us as to what our responses should be.

The Nurse in the opening scene pities her mistress, abandoned by her husband. The Tutor only adds to this by revealing that Medea, already in exile from her native land, is to be exiled again by order of king Creon (70-2). We hear Medea's cries of pain. But we only half hear, if we are in the original unsuspecting audience, the hints that her anger may find its target not in an enemy but in a friend, namely her own children (90-5, cf. 36-7, 112-14).

If we are to approach this play with some of the expectations of that first audience, who saw it in 431 BC, we need to bear in mind what earlier stories about Medea were then current. The story that Medea deliberately killed her children was, when Euripides composed, only a recent innovation. In fact, it was either an innovation by Euripides or by a slightly earlier tragedian called Neophron (this is a very controversial question in scholarship). This was an innovation to the old traditional tale recorded by the Hellenistic scholar Parmeniscus. He said that it was the Corinthians, oppressed by the presence of this foreign sorceress, who rose up against her and killed her children.

A second old version of the plot by an early epic poet called Creophylus made Medea kill both Creon and Jason. Fearing Creon's family, she fled to Athens but had to leave her children behind. They were too young to accompany her, so she left them under the sacred protection of the temple of Hera. Even so, Creon's family killed them and then put about a rumour that, in fact, Medea had committed this sacrilegious act. One or other version of this traditional story still enters the play at its end, when Medea ordains that the Corinthians must institute an annual ritual of atonement for the deaths as if they were themselves responsible for the murder. In fact, according to Parmeniscus' version, a plague followed upon the murders of the children for which the Corinthians had to atone with annual rites. This detail of cult which Euripides could not lightly alter shows more or less what his first audience would have expected to happen in this story.

There was one other version in an old epic poem called the *Korinthiaka*, a poem about Corinth composed by Eumelus of Corinth. Eumelus told the whole story of Jason and the Argonauts' voyage to Colchis and, in this, Medea was misled by a god into killing her children by accident because she had been told she could make them immortal by killing them. Her mistake was obviously meant as a divine punishment for her previous action in persuading the daughters of Pelias to butcher their father on almost the same false pretext, namely that once they chopped him up and popped him in a cauldron she could rejuvenate him, which she then failed to do.

Whichever version of the story of the deaths of Medea's children we knew, we as members of the original audience would not have imagined, even in the darkest corners of our minds, that Medea would deliberately choose to slaughter her own children. For that first audience, Medea is a witch, a sorceress who has killed members of Jason's family out of love for him and caused the death of king Pelias at Iolcus too. But she was not a psychopath towards her own family.

Euripides is careful to ensure that we don't view her in that light. The Nurse and the Tutor both regard her as tragically wronged. Her maltreatment by Jason is only compounded by her exile and that of her children. They fear that she may lash out irrationally in her anger, and so therefore do we, but that is the extent of it.

When Medea appears, the sympathy even of the Chorus is manipulated into complicity with her plans. The women of Corinth see her as an exile with no family to support her, now abandoned by her husband. In a magnificent speech she is careful to enlist their sympathies as one woman to another. She does this by denouncing the norms of contemporary society according to which women were traded like objects, sold by their fathers to a husband whom they did not know, and over whose choice they had no say, in exchange for a dowry. That is not quite the function of a dowry in Greek society – it afforded a certain protection to the woman's family – but that is how she puts it. She would rather, she declares, stand three times in the line of battle than bear one child. The Chorus are persuaded. They offer Medea, as they should and as we would, their sympathy and support. In response to her apparently modest request that they keep silence regarding any revenge she may plot against Jason, they give her the verbal equivalent of a blank cheque. They pledge not to betray her plans, as one would, of course, to someone who had herself been horribly betrayed by Jason. They never suspect that she would or could actually kill her own children to get back at him. Their sympathy is real and so is ours, but Medea will manipulate that sympathy and the playwright will manipulate ours as well.

The next stage in the drama is occasioned by the first of several unexpected but predictable turns of events which further engage sympathy for Medea. King Creon of Corinth, afraid of Medea's magic powers, orders her into exile with her children at once. As if Creon had read his Machiavelli very carefully, he knows that if an absolute ruler cannot either conciliate or dominate those with cause to hate him, he should wipe them out, and he is determined to act accordingly. The immediacy of this demand, its suddenness and the cumulative effect of it coming on top of the facts that Medea is a woman with no rights and now no husband to protect her and her family – all of this produces in the Chorus and in us, quite rightly, an overwhelming feeling of sympathy.

Medea responds by asking Creon for what again seems a very modest favour. Just one day, she asks, this one day in which to arrange her affairs before going into exile for ever with her children. She begs this in the name of the fact that Creon too has children. He has a daughter, and should be able to imagine how she will suffer in exile. Creon is torn. He has suffered, he says, himself for feeling sympathy and mercy before, but he denies that it is in his nature to be tyrannical – he has not really read his Machiavelli. His mercy, though limited, gives us the first pause in granting Medea our sympathy. We realise that Creon is genuinely afraid and acting because of human sympathies of his own, his fear for his own daughter if Medea is around to harm her with the magic powers which he genuinely believes she has. This fear, we begin to suspect, is not entirely irrational. When Creon assents to her modest request, he little knows that his gift of this one day will give Medea enough time to destroy his daughter, his dynasty and himself.

Exit Creon. Medea scornfully asks the Chorus why she would ever have fawned on that man unless she stood to profit by it. We now see that her revenge will carry her along irresistibly, even, as she says, at the cost of her own life, so long as she achieves it. Even so, at least the revenge is proportionate. Jason is certainly culpable. To harm the king and his daughter is at least not to harm people with no involvement in the situation and no responsibility at all for it. However, though the Chorus express no doubts, we have already perhaps become unsure whether we quite approve of her lust for the vengeance and bloodshed which she imagines so vividly and with such relish.

But at once Euripides wrenches our sympathy back towards Medea's side with Jason's appearance. Few more poisonous characters have been created in the whole history of world literature. There are no heroes in this play. The Nurse and the Tutor are humble characters. Creon acts from self-interest that yields to pity. Aegeus is an egoist but a gentleman, as we shall see. But Jason should seem to us, if we have any normal human feelings, to be a heartless and detestable piece of work who even begins by chiding Medea for offending authority when we know, because we have heard Creon say so, that he would have exiled her anyway through fear of her sorcery (285).

I will not dwell on Jason's utter unawareness of how the situation must seem to anyone but an egoist like himself, or his patronising assumption that he conferred on her a great benefit by bringing her to Greece where people behave in the most civilised fashion, to a place where she has fame and a reputation rather than having to live in obscurity. What I want to focus on is how, even with Jason, Medea manipulates his sympathy, and the playwright in turn manipulates ours. In Medea's first scene with him, a 'scene' in the fullest sense of the word, she offers no compromises and denounces him as he deserves. He is thoroughly trounced, yet clearly notices nothing and understands nothing. He thinks at the end that he is being generous and behaving in a proper and gentlemanly manner by merely providing money and letters of introduction to his first family in exile, while he can happily fulfil his ambition to create a second royal family and succeed ultimately to the throne of Corinth. No son of king Creon is ever mentioned in this play, and it was normal in the Greece of the Heroic Age imagined by the dramatist for a kingdom to pass not to the king's son but to the most eligible suitor for the king's daughter. This is what Jason has to lose: his wife is the only obstacle to obtaining a kingdom.

The play is now at an impasse. We see that Medea's will to vengeance is unstoppable but we do not see how she can avoid paying for her vengeance with her own life. Once again, Euripides makes the play take a sudden turn, a turn that as usual affects our view of the characters. That turn is more unexpected than usual. Enter king Aegeus of Athens, one of the few total surprises in Greek tragedy. The playwright has taken an unusual risk, because Aegeus' entry is motivated, it at first seems, by nothing more than sheer coincidence, the coincidence that he is passing through Corinth on his way back from consulting the Delphic oracle. It is only in retrospect that we come to see how profoundly appropriate his entry is. We learn at once why he went to Delphi. He went to ask the oracle how he can have children, because his wife is childless. Here, then, is the motivation. Jason had already thoughtlessly said to Medea at line 565, 'you need no children' (Lattimore's translation). Jason wants new children but evidently cares little for those which he already has; Aegeus has none but desperately wants some. By the same extraordinary coincidence which led Aegeus to Corinth, Medea can, she reveals, solve his problem. She can give him drugs which will end his childlessness. There is a profound irony in her offer to give Aegeus drugs so that he can have children when she is about to use drugs to kill Creon's. But Medea obtains, contrary to all expectation when she saw no way out of the impasse which she faced, something in exchange for this important gift to king Aegeus: as by a sudden inspiration, she asks him, begs him for a safe haven in Athens. When Aegeus learns of her abandonment, her exile and that of her children, he is filled with sympathy and at once promises to receive her there. His reaction confirms that the Chorus and we ourselves were quite right to respond to her situation as we did.

But again, Medea manipulates sympathy. Instead of merely accepting Aegeus' offer, she makes him swear the most terrible and binding oath to receive her in Athens come what may. She explains to him, when he objects, that this is because she is afraid of the forces of king Creon. She fears that she may be extradited back to Corinth. The oath is to be sworn by the earth and the sun.

One who breaks it, it is implied, will be rejected by the entire earth and have no place to go. Wherever he tries to hide, he will not escape vengeance because he will be seen by the all-seeing eye of the sun, the omnipresent ray. (The Greeks thought that you see by a ray coming out of your eye, and compared the sun to such a ray.) Medea had already alluded to her descent from the sun-god, Helios (406), and indeed that god as her grandfather will come to her rescue at the end.

The oath seems excessive even to the unknowing Aegeus, but Medea obliges him to swear. Euripides need not have given us this detail, because we never see Medea flee to Athens as an unholy murderess, nor do we witness any attempts to extradite her, nor any intimidation of the Athenians by the Corinthians on charges of murder.

So why is the scene here? Why are we made to witness the oath? By it, the playwright achieves a number of effects at once. He, of course, reminds us of Medea's connection with Helios which will be important for the close of the play. He emphasises Medea's determination and forcefulness in getting this king to swear. But above all he once again shows us the manipulation of sympathy in action. When Aegeus swears to provide Medea with an inviolable sanctuary, he does so in total ignorance of what she is about to do. Like the Chorus earlier, sworn to silence in the face of whatever Medea might do, like Creon with that one extra single day, Aegeus now signs a blank cheque on which Medea now proceeds to write a sum that no normal individual would pay.

What we, the original audience, may already have known is that, in some versions of the legend, Medea ended up married to Aegeus. I think this story was known to the poet when, at the end, he makes Medea predict that she will live at Athens in Aegeus' house. What else can this mean but her marriage to him? The wife always lived in the house of the husband in Greek society. In this play, then, we actually see Jason destroy his first marriage in a failed attempt to make a second one, and Medea make a second marriage in the process of avenging the termination of her first one.

Only when she knows she has a place to go does she conceive her plan to punish Jason by killing his bride and all who touch her and then killing her own children too. When the Chorus hear of this, they form and echo our own reaction of horror, the shock that her vengeance goes far beyond all proportion, far beyond anything that could be justified. Having manipulated sympathy to achieve this end, Medea is now unredeemable in our eyes, yet we fully understand how she has reached this point.

The next manipulation of a character's sympathy comes when Jason re-enters. Medea has summoned him to ask him to beg Creon for a repeal from exile, not for herself but for their children. A selfless, reasonable request it would seem, a middle way out of the impasse which a different and humbler Medea could have attempted to achieve when Creon first imposed his decree of banishment on her and on the children. But this is, of course, not such a request – however it may seem. Any intelligent man not totally preoccupied by his own egoism would see the falsity of this speech, when Medea says that she ought to have 'joined in the wedding, stood by the bed, taken pleasure in attendance on your bride' (887-8) – exactly what she would find the most galling, the most intolerable, the most outrageous thing to do – actions vividly imagined as if to urge her on in her strategy of deceit towards Jason. But again Jason understands nothing. He even criticises her generosity with her gifts to the bride: the royal house needs no such garments, and if his own bride thinks of him she will value his intercession on behalf of his children more than any gifts. This is right, of course, and true, but this Jason can only see good human motives when they favour what he wants for himself. He is blind to the true motive behind these deadly gifts, especially the crown which brings death to whoever puts it on, as his ambition for the crown of Corinth will bring ruin to all his hopes. But his sympathy is aroused by this apparently selfless request, a request of course that it is astonishing and telling that he did not think to make for himself. He willingly agrees, and as the children leave with their tutor to beg that their banishment be lifted we know that their mission must succeed, that their exile will be annulled, but that their gifts will kill the princess who intercedes on their behalf.

This last manipulation of a character's sympathy, that of the princess, happens offstage in the palace, but even so we are made aware of it. The Tutor enters joyfully with the children to announce their reprieve. This announcement reveals that, once again, Medea has succeeded in exploiting others' sympathy towards her plight. The playwright engineers one of those marvellous scenes (of which his rival, Sophocles, was a master) in which good news is treated with dismay. In fact, the reprieve brings Medea face to face with the reality of her behaviour, that her plan to kill her children to spite her husband will spite herself too. Hatred of others, in short, is also destructive of oneself. We hardly stop to consider, nor could Euripides let us do so, that there is nothing to prevent Medea taking the children to Athens as she once mentions she could (1058). We are given no time to reflect on this possibility, briefly tossed aside, as the drama sweeps on. At once Medea says 'No! No!'

Euripides hides this eventuality, if he needed to, behind the penultimate manipulation of our own sympathy, when Medea is tormented by hesitation as to whether she should go ahead and kill her children. She focuses on the fact that the children will have a city, Corinth, to stay in, but she will not be with them, will never see them grown up and attend on their marriage-bed, in the way she deceitfully suggested she ought to have in the case of Jason's new bride. In short, her jealousy of Jason stops her from letting the children live with him and without her.

So the dreadful news breaks. When revealing her plan, Medea said that her crown and robe would kill all who touched her bride. We in the first audience expected that it would be Jason, whom she had accused in their scene of being obscenely eager to enjoy his new bride in her place. In a version of the tale recorded by the Roman writer Hyginus, the secretary of Augustus, this was what in fact happened. King, princess and Jason – they all met their end in the same way through Medea's gifts. But the Messenger from the palace makes clear that if we expected Jason to be killed in this way we were misled. It is not Jason who embraces the bride and therefore gets consumed by Medea's poison which is burning her to death, but her father, Creon, whose forebodings about his own sympathetic nature when he yielded to Medea's request are now horribly confirmed. In fact, Medea's success in killing Creon recapitulates her earlier feat in killing the wicked king Pelias, to which allusion was made earlier in the play. Pelias' daughters watched Medea chop up a sheep, boil it in a cauldron and have it come out alive and indeed rejuvenated as a lamb. So, when Medea promised the daughters that they could rejuvenate their father if they did the same, they foolishly obeyed. Likewise king Creon is killed via his daughter. Their deaths, of course, are horrible and vividly described by the Messenger. Medea's crown and robe are anointed with a chemical agent whose effects on the human body are very like one of the most inhumane of modern warfare's inventions – napalm.

No audience can hear the Messenger's speech and not feel extreme revulsion towards the cause of all this, yet worse when Medea, in a parody of Greek ideals of heroic manliness, takes up her sword against her own two sons and we hear their screams of death.

In the last scene of the play, Jason, frantic with grief and fear for his children after the assassination of the Corinthian royal family, beats unforgettably against the palace doors to try to save his children from their vengeance, which would represent a return (as we saw) to the traditional story. As usual his problems in fact lie where he never even suspects. He had never even considered the possibility that Medea herself could kill his children to make him suffer a childless old age and an ignoble death, as she predicts, when he is hit by a timber from the rotting *Argo*'s hull.

There is one last manipulation of sympathy to which the playwright subjects us, namely in our view of the gods. At the start of the play, Jason is the one who is punished for breaking his oaths which he had sworn upon his marriage to honour Medea's marriage bed. Medea is loud in her condemnations of this betrayal and we sympathise with her. She makes the Chorus agree to observe silence. She makes Aegeus swear by this most terrible oath on earth and sun to give her sanctuary, and indeed she seems at the beginning of the play to be the innocent, the wronged, the weaker party who has no family to protect her, no native land, she who has lost everything with the loss of her husband, her defender, lost all possibility of having her rights protected. This then leads to a sudden reversal when at the end of the play Medea is the stronger party. In her scene with Jason she actually describes herself as a curse to Jason, but then at the end of the play she is, as it were, magically transformed into a physical embodiment of the curse, a woman who becomes almost one of the Erinyes, the figures who for the Greeks embodied the anger, the rage and the hatred that arise when promises and oaths are broken. Not only has she become this powerful figure from being a wronged and humbled figure, she has acquired almost a divine status. She is shown by the poet as presenting at the end of the play a series of predictions and prophecies. She is rescued by her grandfather Helios in his chariot, allegedly drawn by winged dragons in the first production (and there is actually evidence for this, though I don't expect we'll get such a chariot tonight). She is able not only to predict the future, to predict Jason's death, to predict his suffering, but also her own salvation in Athens, her own marriage to king Aegeus, and ultimately the Corinthians' need to found the cult in atonement for the death of her children. These are things that in Greek drama only gods can do. Only a god can appear at the end to resolve all the things that were not resolved, to predict the future and to bring the storyline into harmony with the traditional tale. Medea does all of these things.

This leaves us with one final problem, one final unexpected turn of events, and one final manipulation of our sympathy. We start out wanting to believe that the gods will actually uphold oaths and support those who have been wronged. Indeed, the sun-god Helios does support Medea, a support which is dramatically demonstrated at the end of the play by her rescue and by the authority with which she can speak towards Jason. But although we wanted the gods to vindicate oaths and justice, what kind of justice is it that we see being vindicated? How can we accept what Medea has actually done, and how can we see the gods as validating that? In short, this is the last, deepest and most troubling of the many questions which Euripides raised and which he liked to bother his audience with. Not only are there no heroes in this play, not only are our sympathies ruthlessly manipulated, but our expectations of what the divine order underlying the world should be are overthrown and we are made to question them. Perhaps it was for this reason that in the original performance of 431 BC the group of three plays in which Medea appeared was awarded by the judges the third out of three prizes. It was not a hit. Perhaps this play was, but the set of plays got the thumbs down from the audience. Euripides did not allow his audiences to be comfortable. He wanted to unsettle them and the audience at the time evidently did not appreciate the experience. I hope it will be different tonight.

Medea and the divided mind

Richard Jenkyns

The role of the Chorus in Greek tragedy is central, so much so that in Aeschylus' *Suppliants*, for example, its lines represent more than half of the play. The stage of the fifth-century Greek theatre was very like this one – barely raised at all above the area known as the orchestra, where the Chorus sang and danced. The presence of the Chorus naturally makes these plays into public dramas. Very rarely is a character alone on the stage (except when he or she gives an introductory speech before the Chorus enter), and some Greek tragedies make a virtue of this public quality. Many of the heroes of Greek tragedy are indeed kings, rulers or leaders of some sort – figures with a public role.

Thus, *Oedipus the King* begins, even before the Chorus have entered, with Oedipus himself appearing and addressing a gathering of suppliants with the words: 'O children (*O tekna*)'. He is the father of his people addressing representatives of the citizens of Thebes as a whole. Similarly in the *Oresteia*, the first play of that trilogy, *Agamemnon*, is clearly a great public drama. The king, Agamemnon, and the queen, Clytemnestra, who is going to murder him, confront one another before the Chorus, the elders of the city of Argos, who can again be seen as representative of the people. What we witness is a grand public confrontation. In the third play of the trilogy, the Chorus are the Furies, and the main action is built around their attempt to destroy Orestes as punishment for his killing of his mother. In this case the Chorus are very obviously major actors in the central conflict of the drama.

The middle play of the trilogy, the *Libation Bearers*, is different in feeling, and of some interest if one is thinking about *Medea*. Unlike the two outer plays, it has the character of a domestic drama, and the Chorus significantly are slave-women – that is, domestics of the household. The two principal characters are not very grand figures, and they are very youthful: the young Orestes and the young Electra. They lean on the older slave-women for advice and support. In this way the nature of the Chorus gives the *Libation Bearers* its distinctive tone and quality.

I said that very rarely is a character alone. One exception is Ajax in Sophocles' play of that name. Most exceptionally, the Chorus depart in the middle of the drama, leaving Ajax entirely alone; and in this solitude he makes his last speech and kills himself. This is a very exceptional scene for a second reason: because he kills himself on stage. Almost all deaths in Greek tragedy – and there are a lot of them – take place off stage. We may hear screams but we do not see the slaughter. Ajax's death is an exception to test the rule.

In the *Agamemnon*, Cassandra is exceptional in another way, one which again is of some interest if we are considering *Medea*. Agamemnon leaves the stage and Clytemnestra is about to follow in order to kill him. But she intends to kill Cassandra, Agamemnon's concubine, also. So she pauses, commanding Cassandra to enter the house. Cassandra does not obey, remaining on stage, and to our surprise the killing is postponed for nearly three hundred lines. Instead, we get (utterly unexpectedly) the most impressive and extraordinary psychological drama in the whole of Greek tragedy. Cassandra begins incoherently. She is not even speaking Greek. From this chaotic utterance she moves into lyric singing and dancing and eventually into spoken words. Finally she comes to an acceptance of her fate and even to the state of pitying others more than she pities herself. The scene is extraordinary because the interior of her mind, as it were, opens out. She is indeed interacting with the Chorus during this scene, but what we witness, in contrast to the public confrontation between Agamemnon and Clytemnestra earlier in the play, is the internal workings of her mind exposed to our gaze or to our hearing. Medea is similarly a person who reveals to us the inner operation of her mind in a famous and powerful soliloquy.

I said that the *Libation Bearers* of Aeschylus was in a sense a domestic drama, but it is only domestic as part of a larger whole. What about *Medea*? Would one describe this as a domestic drama? My answer is going to be: yes and no.

I spoke earlier about the Chorus in Aeschylus partly to set in context the interesting thing that happens to the Chorus in this play of Euripides'. The Chorus now becomes marginal. Almost it seems to be an embarrassment for the playwright. You might think that the Corinthian women would stop Medea killing her children once they had realised that this was their intention, and there is a certain artificiality in their not doing so. Something similar happens in another of Euripides' plays, *Hippolytus*, where the Chorus learn that Phaedra, who has fallen incestuously in love with her own stepson, is going to tell a lie, once she has learnt that he will not give way and reciprocate her passion. This lie will bring about his death. But the Chorus have been sworn to secrecy and therefore cannot say anything – a rather transparent plot device. In the production that we are about to see, the Chorus is to be played by a single person, and interestingly enough, I think we shall find that this works with *Medea* very well. A year ago, when I last came to see the Actors of Dionysus, the work was *Oedipus the King*, and there the words of the Chorus were spread between three or four different people. Again, in such a public drama, that solution seemed right. But to regard the Chorus in tonight's play simply as a person who happens to be a confidante of the heroine is likely to work because of this drama's newly private character.

In some ways one can see *Medea* as having moved a long way from the origins of Greek tragedy in choral dance and singing. Yet in another way I suggest that it can be seen as going back to the style and method of Euripides' older contemporary Sophocles, because of the eighteen or nineteen plays by Euripides that survive this is the only one that is dominated throughout by one great human figure. I have included the word 'human' for the sake of another case that I want to come to in a moment. The grandly dominant protagonist was a common figure in Sophocles' plays. Anyone who has seen *Oedipus Tyrannus* knows that it is dominated by the power and will of a single figure, Oedipus, and one may say the same of Ajax in the play that bears his name. One of Sophocles' last plays, *Philoctetes*, is concentrated on the hero in a rather different way.

What is distinctive about *Medea* can also be seen by thinking about one or two features of Greek drama which we have come to take for granted but which are actually rather odd. One is that virtually all these plays are myths, set in a mythical age. Of the 32 Greek tragedies that survive more or less complete, only one, the oldest of all, does not have a mythical setting and plot: Aeschylus' *Persians*, about a recent historical event. Otherwise they are all mythology through and through. When you think about it, this is a pretty remarkable fact. No plays about the

Greeks' glorious achievements in historical times? Only *Persians*? How surprising!

Another distinctive feature of Greek tragedy is that it deals mostly with heroic or royal figures. Even though *Medea* has a domestic character, the protagonist is the daughter of a king and Jason is about to desert her to marry the daughter of another king. Moreover, these plays are full of gods. Many of them actually have gods as characters, and in those that do not there is usually a great deal of talk about the gods, so that we are constantly aware of their controlling or directing the way in which the story unfolds. But in *Medea* mostly (though not entirely) the gods seem absent.

What we find in this play is a kind of tension between something grand (Medea is extraordinary and special, as we realise at the end: she is the grand-daughter of the Sun, who lends her his chariot) and something domestic (the story is about a woman – as it were any woman, even if a powerful and strong-willed woman – who has been deserted by her husband).

Another way of bringing out what is distinctive about *Medea* is to think about the characteristic structure of Euripides' works and to consider in what ways this play is like and unlike the others. He commonly began with a single character speaking the prologue. This character might be a god or a ghost or a human being. Quite commonly he ended with the *deus ex machina* – the device by which a god or goddess appears and sorts out the business of the story at the end. We know rather little directly about how plays were staged in the fifth century: most of our evidence is of later date. We do know that in the fifth century there was a kind of crane which swung the character on to the stage so that the god or goddess appeared above the human actors. But exactly how it worked we are not sure.[1] That need not matter much, provided that we can grasp the dramatic effect. Let us take an example: in *Hippolytus*, the goddess Aphrodite appears at the very beginning and declares that she is going to destroy Hippolytus because he does not respect her. At the end of the play, the goddess Artemis appears on the machine and brings the action to its conclusion. And thus, although this is a pro-

---

[1] In Aristophanes' *Peace* (421 BC) the device is parodied when Trygaeus flies to heaven on a giant dung beetle. At one point, overcome by fear of falling, he even addresses the crane operator (174ff.).

foundly human drama, it is framed by a pair of divine powers. That expresses a part of the play's meaning: human life is indeed framed by the divine, which is above and beyond it.

The character who speaks the prologue, and even the character on the machine, is not necessarily a god. In *Hecuba* the prologue is spoken by the ghost of a murdered man, in *Electra* by a humble farmer. Similarly, in *Medea* it is not a great god or hero who speaks the prologue, but the Nurse, affectionate, sad, grumbling, an ordinarily human and literally domestic figure. But the great *coup de théâtre* comes when the *deus ex machina* appears: the god on the machine – except that it isn't. The figure aloft is, to our amazement, Medea herself, in a chariot borrowed from a god. People sometimes say that Medea has become a god. That seems to me to be quite untrue, even speaking metaphorically. She is still entirely human: the spectacular effect is that where we expect to see a god we see human Medea instead, and this greatly influences our final assessment of the tragedy as a whole, by emphasising the way in which this single figure dominates the entire work.

At this point let us bring into view another play of Euripides' in which something comparable and yet unlike happens: *Bacchae*. This time the dominant figure is the god Dionysus. Dionysus speaks the prologue, in which he says that he will make the city of Thebes obey him. He reveals that he will enter the action; this he does by confronting Pentheus, the king of Thebes, in a series of three scenes. We then hear that he has brought about the hideous death of Pentheus, after which he appears on the machine at the end to sort out the action and bring the play to its resolution. The whole play is thrilled through by this single figure, this nature-god who fills the whole of nature and fills the whole of the play. *Bacchae*, then, is saturated in a sense of the divine.

One only has to describe that to see how different tonight's play is, for whereas *Bacchae* is god-filled, *Medea* is Medea-filled. This is a play in which there is remarkably little about the gods. I stressed earlier how prominent the gods are in Greek tragedy, either as actual characters or in the mouths of others, to bring out the difference from what we have meet here. It is not that this is an anti-god play. That would be an entirely anachronistic thought. Again, I would compare *Hippolytus*, where the goddess Artemis, to whom Hippolytus has devoted his life, appears at the end, and the dying man realises how little she cares about his death. He very simply says, 'Go on your way rejoicing, blessed maiden; easily you leave our long companionship.'

I think that it is wrong to see that as a reproach. One has to turn the Christian idea on its head. The Christian idea is that God loves us and that God's capacity for love is part of his greatness. The Greek idea is almost the opposite of that. What makes the gods gods is that they don't have to care about us. We don't matter to them, and therefore are they gods. Their insouciance is the essence of their divinity. One can see what is not in *Medea* by contrasting it with Seneca's reworking of the play. His own *Medea* was written in the first century AD. In its very last line, Jason shakes his fist, as it were, and declares, 'Bear witness wherever you go that there are no gods.' But that kind of nihilism is quite alien to Euripides.

Another way of bringing out the character and quality of Euripides is to compare the melodramatic *coup de théâtre* with which Seneca ends: he has Medea toss the bodies of the dead children down to Jason as a last hideous taunt. If you set that against the ending of the earlier play, you will see, I hope, how much more psychological truth there is in Euripides, because Jason asks at least to have the chance to bury his children, and Medea realises that the best kind of revenge is not to allow this. Euripides' version is also psychologically true in understanding that even though she has killed the children, she still wants to keep them. She is still their mother, and in a perverse and ghastly way she is still cherishing them.

Although she is a very powerful character, she is not a superwoman. It was essential to many of the stories told about Medea in other places that she was a witch and possessed all kinds of magical powers. That element is not totally suppressed by Euripides, but he plays it down. The so-called feminism in this play also points to the same moral. In some famous passages she speaks not as a superhuman figure but as a woman about the vulnerability of women – for example, when she says that marriage is everything to a woman, since the woman's place is indoors, whereas if a man is unhappy in his domestic life he can go out into the open air, meet his friends and cheer himself up (230ff.). The Chorus similarly say that the world is turning upside-down, the rivers are running back to their sources, honour is coming to the race of women: in other words, impossible things are happening (410ff.).

61

One naturally thinks of tragedy as being concerned with conflict between powerful wills, but one might well ask if anything
of that is to be found in this play? Doesn't Medea have it rather
easy? She brings about the death of the princess Glauce, and the
management of this seems to give her little trouble. She wraps
around her little finger Aegeus, king of Athens, from whom she
needs to extract a promise of safe haven, so that she will have a
refuge after committing her murders. He is important, incidentally,
because he puts into her head the notion of killing the children. The
moment when he reveals that he is childless is pivotal, as it gives
the idea of how she can revenge herself upon Jason.

Jason himself is a cheap and contemptible figure, but
Euripides' portrait is psychologically brilliant. His first words are
the statement that he thinks that anger is a very bad thing. We
realise that he has come with his words prepared, and I think
that our likely reaction to this opening sentence is to say to
ourselves, 'Yes and no.' Of course, anger is a bad thing. On the
other hand, to possess passion seems much better than to be
passionless and smooth and to have one's words off pat like Jason
himself. Jason pretends to be kind and generous. 'Even if you
hate me,' he says, 'I couldn't think badly of you' (463-4). One
resists that. It is not that he is honourably forgiving; rather, one
feels, he is such a creep that he doesn't have any strong feelings
at all. Indeed, he may inspire the sense that there is a kind of
virtue in anger. A little later, when he is arguing with Medea, he
says, 'I need, it seems, to be good at talking' (522). Again, he has
revealed a moral deficiency: he thinks that having the ready
words rather than true feelings is what is important. The Chorus'
response a little later still is interesting. In a simple but effective
way they say, 'You have adorned your words very finely, and yet
it seems to me you have betrayed your wife and acted unjustly'
(576-8). He thinks about the glib language to cover up what is
wrong. By contrast, Medea wants to get to the heart of things.

The reason that Medea's adversaries are represented as people
whom she can easily defeat, deceive and triumph over is that her
great adversary is herself. Here we need to look back right to the
beginnings of Greek literature: to Homer's *Iliad*. Aeschylus is
supposed to have said that his plays were merely slices cut from
the great banquet of Homer. Presumably what he did not mean
is that he got the plots from Homer, because rather few Greek
tragedies have their plots taken from Homer. What I think that

he meant (or the inventor of the anecdote meant) was that Homer created the tragic idea and that Achilles is a great tragic hero. In the ninth book of the *Iliad*, when some of his fellow Achaeans are trying to persuade Achilles to give up his wrath and return to battle and Ajax urges him to think of his friends, Achilles replies, 'Everything that you say is in a way according to my spirit (*thumos*), but my heart swells with rage when I think of the way that Agamemnon has insulted me.' Here is something remarkable and unexpected so early in the literature of Europe. For Homer, the intelligence and moral life of the protagonist are important. That is not generally a characteristic of early heroic poetry. In the great German myth Siegfried has no inner life of interesting complexity: the point is that he is a man who is wholly ignorant of the world, who does not know what fear is, and has never seen a woman. Or if you read an Icelandic saga you will find no concern with the interior lives of the characters: the power lies in the plain telling of outward action. But Homer is interested in the inside of his hero's mind: Achilles looks inside himself and he finds two emotions. He says, 'On the one hand I like what you say.' That is one emotion. 'On the other hand I have this anger.' That is another emotion. In other words, he sees a division of emotions within his mind.

That is the ultimate origin of the idea of division that we find within the mind of Medea. The difference is that what Achilles sees is two things fixed inside him, while what Euripides explores is a mind that wavers. In Medea's great soliloquy we hear her changing her mind back and forth, fluctuating until she comes to a final decision. Almost at the end of that soliloquy she says, 'My *thumos*, my passionate spirit, is stronger than my reasoned thoughts' (1079).

This conflict or division of mind is one between reason and passion, and it is what made the play so immensely influential on the literature of the succeeding centuries. Later generations found the divided mind psychologically fascinating in itself, and they were especially intrigued by the play's concentration on the interior processes of a woman, someone who seems naturally vulnerable but proves to be powerful. There was also a growing interest in love as a literary theme, though in Euripides' play this concerns not so much Medea herself as Glauce and Jason. So it is no accident that in the best epic poem of the next few centuries, the *Argonautica* of Apollonius of Rhodes (between 150 and 200 years later than Euripides' play), the most interesting character is not Jason but Medea, and the focus is upon her divided mind, torn between loyalty to her father and her country on the one hand and her love for Jason on the other.

Later still, the study of the divided mind crossed into Latin poetry. In the middle of the first century BC, at the heart of the longest poem by Catullus is Ariadne, a woman in distress because she has betrayed her father and country for love, and then been deserted by her lover in turn. Virgil greatly admired this poem, and echoed some of Ariadne's words and sentiments when he wrote Dido's passionate speeches in the fourth book of the *Aeneid*. From there the theme passed on to Ovid: in the middle books of his *Metamorphoses* there is a series of divided-mind heroines, whose mental conflict is often caused by an illicit passion. One such case is Scylla, who betrays her father and her city to the enemy leader, with whom she is in love. Another of Ovid's stories concerns a woman who is in love with her own father and is therefore torn between passion and morality. There are two stories of lesbian amours; one of which ends tragically, the other happily, because the metamorphosis in this case consists in the infatuated woman being changed into a man. Among Ovid's conflicted heroines is Medea herself, and it is into her mouth that he places the famous words that describe the conflict in a nutshell: *'video meliora proboque, deteriora sequor'* ('I see the better course and approve it, but I follow the worse', *Metamorphoses* 7.20-1) It is similar to the sentiment expressed by St Paul in his Epistle to the Romans: 'For the good that I would I do not, but the evil which I would not, that I do.'

St Paul was referring to a famous philosophical puzzle, one that arose in the fifth century BC, in Euripides' lifetime: how can it be that a person does wrong, knowing it to be wrong? Euripides was part of the great philosophical and intellectual ferment of his time. Socrates had posed the puzzling question, and answered it with the celebrated Socratic paradox: no one willingly does wrong. All wrongdoing is in fact some kind of mistake. Socrates' pupil Plato and Plato's pupil Aristotle also worried at the question, searching for what they hoped might be better answers, but to go into that would take us too far from *Medea*. Let it suffice to say that in literary terms this play stands at the head of the long history of poets – and much later, novelists – exploring the psychology of the divisions that we all experience between reason, will and desire.

HIPPOLYTUS

Hippolytus, 2004. Leila Crerer as Phaedra;
Roger Ringrose as Theseus.
Photo: daveashtonphotography.com

In 428 BC Euripides was awarded first prize for his trilogy and satyr play, of which *Hippolytus* is the only play to survive. This was Euripides' second play called *Hippolytus*, and what we hear about the first version suggests that there Phaedra was portrayed as a predatory female in the tradition of Potiphar's wife.

Hippolytus was one of **aod**'s earliest productions (1993). Since then they have taken it on the road in 1999 and, in an adapted version, in 2004.

Guide to mythological detail

The mythical setting for the play is quite complicated and revealed piecemeal. A 'timetable' for the plot might run something like this:

1. Hippolytus was the son of Theseus and 'the Amazon' (307, 351, not named in the play, but called Hippolyte [as in the Penguin translation] or Antiope). His status as a *nothos* (bastard) is made clear by 309.
2. Hippolytus was brought up in Trozen by his great-grandfather Pittheus (Theseus was son of Aithra, daughter of Pittheus).
3. Theseus later married Phaedra and they had two children (Akamas and Demophon, neither named in the play, but mentioned by the Nurse in 305ff.). The Nurse's words imply that they are legitimate and in line to succeed to the throne.
4. Hippolytus came to Athens from Trozen for the Mysteries (24ff.). Aphrodite made Phaedra fall in love with him and she set up a temple to Aphrodite ('at Hippolytus') at the foot of the Acropolis.
5. Theseus killed his cousins, the sons of Pallas who had attacked him since they disputed his right to succeed Aegeus.

67

6. Theseus and Phaedra left Athens for Trozen to spend a year in exile because of the pollution caused by the killing of kin (34-7). Phaedra is overwhelmed by her passion for Hippolytus. She has not eaten for three days (275).

7. When the play opens Theseus is abroad (281 we learn he is abroad, 792 + 807 that he has returned, garlanded, from an oracle), but he returns in line 790 to find Phaedra dead.

8. All the events in the play take place (as usual) on one day, as Aphrodite ominously announces in lines 22 and 57 and others echo (Chorus 368-70, Phaedra 726, Theseus 889-90).

9. After Hippolytus' death he had a precinct at Trozen containing a temple of Aphrodite and a hero-cult in which girls about to marry lamented for him and offered him their hair (1423-30; cf. Pausanias 2.32.1).

Note: Theseus has a double paternity in the play: normally Aegeus is said to be his father (1281 Artemis addresses him as 'Theseus, royal son of Aegeus', but when he delivers the curse, then he calls upon Poseidon as his father). It is also assumed that Theseus is ruler of Trozen as well as Athens.

Why does Hippolytus reject sex?[1]

Richard Seaford

Hippolytus is about celibacy and its disastrous consequences. We regard sex as an internal pressure, whereas for the Greeks sex is projected onto the goddess Aphrodite. It is an *external* pressure. So, when Hippolytus rejects Aphrodite and declines to follow her, he is rejecting sex for himself. A central question is: Why did he do that? What does it mean that Hippolytus rejects sex? One has to think hard about this and perform an informed effort of the imagination because celibacy means something very different to us from what it would have meant in fifth-century Athens. If you ask the question, 'Were Greek males celibate?', 'Did they abstain from sex?', then one can think of three ways in which they abstained from sex.

One is ritual purity. That is to say, we know that people performing priestly office might for a period be required to abstain from sexual relations, in particular before certain sacrifices. We know that there were sanctuaries which it was undesirable to enter if one had had sexual relations. In that category, sexuality is a distraction or an impurity which will stand in the way of your relationship with the deity.

The second way in which ancient Greek males might have abstained from sex is by virtue of their desire to be in control of themselves. Greek citizens were very insistent on their freedom, and that means not just their freedom from tyrants but freedom from passion, which is a central theme of philosophy. If you are subject to your passions you are not really free. So control of the self by the self was a reason why, if you were a Greek man, you might abstain from sexual relations, or at least certain kinds of sexual relations.

The third way in which abstention from sex might be important to a Greek male is rather more complex. It is something which is implied for the first time in Plato in the fourth century

[1] This talk was delivered extempore, recorded and transcribed.

BC, which is after the great period of Athenian tragedy, and it involves thinking of yourself as divided into parts. So, there is within you an immortal part, the intellect or the soul. And there is also a corporeal part, the body, and the corporeal part has these physical appetites such as sex. It is subject to the impressions of the senses, whereas the immortal part, the soul, should be free from those things, and contemplates those things in the world which are permanent and eternal. The world, too, is divided into parts, and there are in the world the things that the senses perceive and those as well which the mind and soul perceive. What the senses perceive is changeable and what the mind or the soul perceives is permanent and eternal.

You will see from *Hippolytus* that Hippolytus is interested in not one of these things. True, purity is important to Hippolytus, but it is not really ritual purity, and it is not a negative purity. Paradoxically, there is nothing negative about Hippolytus' rejection of sex. What he wants clearly is a kind of purity which consists of his communion with the goddess Artemis, the virgin goddess who was the embodiment of female asexuality. For example, he brings her a crown plucked from the pure meadow (73-81). So this rejection of sex is associated with the purity of nature as well as with the goddess Artemis. All those three kinds of rejection of sexuality I mentioned are negative. They are rejecting the destructiveness of sexuality, whereas Hippolytus is engaged in what one might call positive purity.

Moreover, those three kinds of what I called celibacy are not really celibacy. They are just abstention from sex. Ritual purity for the ancient Greeks was just a temporary abstention from sex. It was not a way of life. Rejection of the corporeal world did not actually mean celibacy for life, it just meant temporary abstention from sex or abstention from a certain kind of sex: the kind of sex that controlled you, rather than you controlling it.

For celibacy as a way of life, as something entirely positive, we have to wait for Christianity. All three of the reasons I have given feed into Christianity along with a number of others. Our notion of celibacy is clearly coloured by Christian celibacy and in order to understand *Hippolytus*, you have to rid yourself of any preconceptions, because something very different is going on in *Hippolytus*. What is it? What does it mean?

Theseus, Hippolytus' father, who gets very upset with Hippolytus, seems to have a vague idea about this, because he says

70

at one point, 'Go off and honour Lord Orpheus. Be a vegetarian, and honour empty writings' (952-4). What does he mean by that? He is referring to something known as the Orphic cult, and we know that in the Orphic cult vegetarianism was practised.

We also know that the Orphics, so-called, believed in reincarnation, and that may have been associated with their vegetarianism in the sense that, if you ate an animal, you might be eating your great-grandfather, who might have been reincarnated as an animal.

We also know that the Orphics believed that the immortal soul was imprisoned in the body. We are a combination of a body that will perish and the immortal soul, and that is the first example of that belief which is so thoroughly fundamental to the Christian culture. It occurs first in the Orphics, and Plato, who elaborates this belief giving it an ethical content as well, was clearly influenced by the Orphic belief.

The question, then, is: did the Orphics recommend abstention from sexuality? That would fit very well, because it would explain why Theseus accuses Hippolytus of being an Orphic. The answer is, we don't really have any evidence for that. Such a prohibition might be thought to be consistent with their general outlook, but there is no real evidence (apart, possibly, from this passage in the play).

But clearly Orphism is irrelevant in a sense to the play, because clearly Theseus has got it wrong, Hippolytus is *not* a follower of Orpheus. It is as if Theseus is trying to explain why his son is so odd, and he imagines him to belong to an Orphic sect, which is marginal and esoteric, outside the religion of the city-state. Clearly Theseus has not understood why Hippolytus is as he is. Vegetarianism, of which Theseus accuses Hippolytus, is barely consistent with hunting, and Hippolytus is a hunter. His hunting is at the centre of the play.

This might give us a clue about why Hippolytus is celibate. Humankind for 98% of its existence has been a hunter-gatherer, and hunting is often associated with abstention from sex. Why should that be? It is partly because the band of hunters in a hunter-gatherer society often leaves the centre where the women are and goes for weeks into the wild. It has also been suggested that the aggression needed for hunting derives in part from sexual frustration. Sexual frustration in the male produces aggression, so abstention from sex is just good for hunting.

71

So, one of the reasons why Hippolytus abstains from sex may be to do with hunting. In one of the very earliest narratives, perhaps *the* earliest narrative, the Epic of Gilgamesh, the hunter Enkidu runs with the animals. But when he has sex with a prostitute, the animals abandon him. He can no longer run with the animals because he has become alienated from nature through his sexuality.

As for Greek society at the time of Euripides' *Hippolytus*, hunting had ceased to be a main economic activity. Hunting was very marginal, as it is nowadays. It had more symbolic than economic value. So, what are we to make of this? Myth – and *Hippolytus* is a myth – frequently goes back hundreds or thousands of years into pre-history, and that is why we find so many myths to do with hunting, because hunting is our past as a species. So, the myths of hunting in the Classical period of Greek civilisation may tell you quite a lot about pre-history as they reach back into the past from which they are orally transmitted.

The answer, then, to the question, 'What is this celibacy about?', is that it is just a myth. It has no relation to Greek life of the city-state in which men just weren't celibate and all men expected to practise sex. But of course a myth must mean something. There is so much in our culture that is meaningless that it is easy to forget that all the action on the stage of Dionysus in Athens meant something. Myths wouldn't have survived, they would not have been dramatised unless they had some sort of meaning. So we are still back with the question, 'What does Hippolytus' celibacy in this myth actually mean?'

How many males in myth reject sex in this way? Hippolytus is pretty unusual if not unique in this respect. In Greek myth, it's the females who tend to reject sexual contact, females like Atalanta and Callisto, young women who reject sexuality and rush into the wild and become hunters even. There are also Artemis and Athena, goddesses who reject sexuality. The Greek male gods don't reject sexuality. As far as I know, all those gods, Zeus, Apollo, Dionysus, might be expected to have sex with mortal women. They are just like the ordinary Greek male. There is no question of them not having sex. But for the female goddesses, their whole being, the being of Artemis is defined by her virginity.

I want to look now at Artemis to give us a clue to our answer, because she of course is central to this play. She is the goddess whom Hippolytus worships, just as he rejects Aphrodite. Now, Artemis is a permanent virgin and she is also a huntress, and this is significant because, in being a permanent virgin, she is the reverse of what every Greek girl experienced. Every Greek girl would be expected to get married. There was no question of female celibacy either as a way of life. So Artemis is the reversal of the norm. She is also a huntress, and nothing less female for the Greeks could be imagined. Greek women did not hunt. She also as a huntress belongs to the wild, to the periphery. That too is a reversal of where the woman belongs. The woman belongs in the home, enclosed. What I am suggesting to you is that Artemis represents the reversal of the norm in various codes: in the question of sexuality, because she remains a virgin; in activity, because she is a huntress; and in the spatial code because she belongs in the periphery, whereas the woman belongs in the centre, enclosed at home.

Why does this happen? What does this mean, this central feature of Greek religion that we find not only in this case but in so many others? I now have to talk about ritual, and the fact that young Greek girls, as a preparation for marriage, would have to undergo certain rites of passage in which frequently they went into the periphery, the wild, became like animals; and, of course, they were virgins. In all these respects they were like the goddess Artemis. It is a characteristic of the rite of passage, and particularly for rites of passage into adulthood which this is, that the norms of society are inverted. The girls invert the norms of society. When they are virgins they go hunting and stay on the periphery, and then finally they are reincorporated into society. They move out, experience a period of liminality and then move back again to be incorporated into the norms of society.

Artemis, you might say, is the projection of this state of liminality out on the periphery. She is the immortal embodiment of what happens to many Greek girls in the period before marriage. She, of course, differs from mortal girls because she is never married. That state ends for mortal girls. It doesn't end for Artemis. She is the permanent projection of the state of reversal, and this is very important for understanding so much in Greek culture. It is rather difficult for us because we don't have rites of passage any more. Part of our problem is that we don't have rites of passage. People don't know whether they are children or grown-ups. But for the Greeks these rituals define their lives, in particular I think for a Greek female. There are, of course, certain remnants: stag nights, degree ceremonies. Even the marriage ceremony is a rite of passage. But a difference between the modern marriage and a Greek marriage is that the Greek girl was meant to be reluctant. The rite of passage for the Greeks involves a tension, a contradiction, and that is expressed dramatically sometimes in the wedding in tears, abduction and so on, so as to be overcome. Because it is expressed, it can be overcome. The girl finally is incorporated into the new home which she has never visited before.

Artemis, then, is important as an expression of this tension, this contradiction. She somehow embodies the desire of the virgin to remain a virgin forever, which of course the human being can't but Artemis can. She is therefore a kind of fantasy and she grows out of this situation of tension and contradiction, and the girls feel they have to sacrifice to this deity if they are going to move on. That expresses the importance of the tension, the contradiction. They can't just leave this state without a ritual, and a ritual has to have a deity. The deity is Artemis, because Artemis is resentful of the girl for moving on, because the girl is leaving her sphere of virginity. So, I am explaining a goddess in terms of a human ritual and a human contradiction which is right at the centre of the lives of those people. This is how the goddess then emerges. She is the permanent embodiment of the desire of the girl to remain a virgin. Internal contradictions are frequently expressed externally by the Greeks. They create gods who can contradict each other. The two deities who preside over this situation of contradiction are Artemis and Aphrodite, because the girl is moving from virginity to sexuality. And those are the two deities who in a sense dominate this drama that we are going to see.

Hippolytus is a young man. Young men also went through these rites of passage. They went out into the wilds, hunted for a time, did without sex, went through various inversions of the norm and finally came back as full adult members of the community. We are getting closer to the answer to our question. Hippolytus seems to represent the male in that period of his life. That is to say, hunting in the periphery, abstaining from sex. Like Artemis, Hippolytus seems to want to do that permanently. That makes him rather special.

You have the ritual and you have the myth, and the myth goes to extremes: Artemis and Hippolytus. The difference is, of course, that Hippolytus unlike Artemis is a mortal, so he can't be a permanent virgin, though that is what he seems to want. So, he too like Artemis is in a sense the embodiment of a ritual, the embodiment of a transition, the embodiment of a contradiction. But he is mortal, so he dies, and being a mortal, his devotion to this purity is dangerous. It is, as I said earlier, a positive purity. At one point he says to his father, 'I have a virgin soul' (*parthenos psyche*, 1006).

But that is dangerous for the city-state. Hippolytus is one of those many characters who is in a sense sympathetic, but also thoroughly dangerous for the community. Why? Because the city-state takes its reproduction far more seriously than we can imagine. We actually don't worry about our community dying out because we are not reproducing. Quite the reverse. Most people believe that there are too many people in the world and the less we reproduce the better. But if you are a Greek in a city-state in the fifth century BC it is absolutely vital that the city can reproduce itself for survival, for warfare, for dominating the slaves, for doing the agriculture. It was a relatively small society. The number of male citizens in Athens at the time of Hippolytus was something like forty to fifty thousand. That is why the city puts on these rituals, these rites of passage preparing the girls and the young men for marriage. This is a concern for the *polis*. So, as well as being a projection of ritual, Hippolytus is also a danger for the city-state, because he is putting himself outside this process of reproduction.

There are two points in the play at which this is made sense of in terms of the story. For example, when Hippolytus is defending himself to his father in that pathetic scene he says, 'I can't speak to the masses. I can speak to a few friends, but I can't speak to large numbers of people' (986-7). That would ring an alarm bell for the Greek audience, because he is putting himself outside political life and if you are a Greek you shouldn't do that.

Another point is when Hippolytus, a little later, sees that everything is lost, he says, 'May none of my friends be illegitimate' (1083). The Greek word is *nothos*, bastard. At that point we are reminded that Hippolytus is illegitimate, because he is the son of Theseus and the Amazon Hippolyta, who was a girl-friend of Theseus. Theseus is now married to Phaedra, Hippolytus' step-mother. So Hippolytus is outside the legitimate family, and in fifth-century Athens that would put him at a disadvantage in

75

the *polis* as a somewhat marginal character. We are reminded of that again at the end of the play when there is a further allusion to this marginal state of Hippolytus which puts him outside the *polis* even though he is a member of the royal family. So a dramatic sense is made of the way in which Hippolytus is outside the whole process of the *polis* reproducing itself.

I should say that Orphics too put themselves outside the *polis* by their vegetarianism. If you were a vegetarian in ancient Greek society, you were rejecting animal sacrifices. It isn't just ethical, it is political. You are saying you don't belong to this system which sacrifices animals and is in a sense founded on the ritual of sacrificing animals.

What Hippolytus represents then is the tragic hero who, as is so often the case with the tragic hero, dies piteously, engages our sympathy, but from the point of view of the community, it is good that he is dead. That is a very frequent form of tragedy. You have characteristically this movement from the royal family imploding, destroying itself as occurs in this play, often through murder (here the deaths of Hippolytus and Phaedra) – that typical theme of tragedy is often followed at the end of the tragedy by the founding of a cult for the whole *polis*. So you have a typical movement from the old royal family killing itself (and we sympathise greatly with the fact that these great people should suffer so much), and then at the end of the tragedy a *polis* cult is established which will be permanent, and that ties the action we are seeing on the stage from the mythical past to the present of the audience, because the audience are familiar with these cults. So the action of the mythical past impinges directly onto the experience of the audience, because they know the cult which was founded, and is still going on, and, in contrast to what we are seeing on stage, is permanent, is good, expresses the solidarity of the citizens and expresses the survival of the city-state.

At the end of this play, Artemis comes on and announces the foundation of the cult. She says, 'compensating for what you have suffered, Hippolytus, for ever and ever the virgins of the city will cut their hair for you and lament for you before their marriage' (1423-7). So this confirms what I have been saying that this is one of those rituals of the *polis* in which the young girls are being prepared for marriage, and which express tension and contradiction in the cult from which the figure of Hippolytus emerges, in which the myth emerges from the cult.

In this case the tension and the contradiction within marriage are expressed in the fact that the young women are lamenting for Hippolytus. Young women before marriage may well lament. They are losing their only home to go to a house where they will be under the control of a strange and possibly cruel master. Young women in the wedding, the brides, lament. But in this case the lamentation is, as it were, sublimated, because they are lamenting for Hippolytus. Their tears which are really for themselves are for the figure of Hippolytus, just as Plato said about tragedy, 'we see the tragedy and we shed tears, but the tears are really for ourselves'.

Forces at work in *Hippolytus*

Kenneth Dover

When this play begins, you are confronted by a single figure who tells you what the situation is and also makes some statements about what is going to happen in the play. The figure who speaks this prologue is Aphrodite. She is a goddess, also very commonly called '*Kupris*' by the Greeks because there was a myth that she was born out of the sea on the coast of Cyprus.

This idea of having a god or goddess come before the audience to put them in the picture and sometimes also predict what is going to happen is quite a favourite technique of Euripides'. It is a technique which was taken up and used also a hundred years later in the New Comedy by playwrights like Menander.

First of all, about the present situation: Theseus, the legendary Athenian hero, has a son, Hippolytus, by his first marriage. His second marriage is to Phaedra. Phaedra falls madly in love with her step-son, Hippolytus. She conceals her emotion. Hippolytus, we are told in the prologue, is intensely hostile to Aphrodite. That is to say, he is obsessively hostile to sex.

Then Aphrodite goes on to tell us something of what is going to happen in the play. Theseus is going to curse his son, Hippolytus, and this will cause Hippolytus' death. Phaedra also meets her death, but Aphrodite says, 'Well, I'm not bothered about her.' This prediction, this statement about what is going to happen, is in many ways misleading, partly by omission, because Aphrodite does not tell us anything about what is one of the mainsprings of the plot of the play – that is, that Phaedra's old nurse, against Phaedra's wishes, tells Hippolytus that Phaedra is in love with him. Also (something that is quite significantly misleading, I think) Aphrodite says, 'I will reveal the situation to Theseus' (42). Now, this is misleading in a way because it suggests that she is going to *tell* Theseus about it, but what she means by 'I shall reveal it' is 'I shall cause a sequence of events which will cause Theseus to know about it'. This is the kind of thing that we not infrequently find in a Euripidean prologue. He

78

may sometimes mislead us a bit, so that what actually happens comes as something new and surprising.

About Aphrodite. She is the goddess whom the Romans called Venus, and she is commonly referred to as the goddess of love. Among other things, this expression 'of' needs a bit of explaining, as no doubt many a modern philosopher would say: what does one mean by saying that a deity is the god or goddess 'of' such-and-such? In some cases it is quite obvious. For example, the god Ares. He is the god of war, in the sense that he tirelessly enjoys and promotes war. He could also be thought of as the embodiment or personification of war. And sometimes you have abstractions. One of the most obvious ones is Peace, who is really simply a personification of a state of affairs. These personifications are very vivid in Greek poetry, and to judge from dedications and inscriptions that we find from ancient Greece, they are pretty vivid to the ordinary population too. You can perfectly well address prayers to Peace, or prayers to Good Order. There is no limit to what the Greeks are prepared to personify.

When it comes to Love, the English vocabulary and the Greek vocabulary are very different, because the Greeks divide up the phenomenon rather differently from the way we divide it up. In English, we can speak of love, lust, sex. Of those three words, I am rather fond of the word 'lust'. Among other things, it is only one syllable, whereas 'sexual desire' is five syllables, and I always prefer short words. And, of course, lust is, when you stop to think of it, a necessary condition of procreation, and therefore a necessary condition of the survival of the human race. (I suppose in 1999, that is not absolutely true, but that is rather a new phenomenon, of which the Greeks were unaware.)

In modern English, the word 'love' is used with a fantastic extension: on the one hand, 'love thy neighbour as thyself'; on the other hand, it would be perfectly good contemporary English to say, 'I love making love in a taxi'. There is an old rhyme too from my parents' generation which ran: 'You may love a screeching owl; you may not love a roasted fowl.' Now, love, I think, is quite easily defined. It is the state in which you treat somebody else's security and happiness and well-being as more important than your own. One could say it is as simple as that, however difficult in application.

The meaning of the word 'sex', of course, has changed quite a lot in contemporary English. In many ways it has been replaced nowadays by 'gender'. This is something which to my generation is quite difficult to get used to, because I have always thought of gender as an attribute of nouns, adjectives, pronouns and participles, and sex as an attribute of living animals and plants (in most cases, two sexes for each species, but just occasionally, in unusual species, three or four). I think this shift of words and the prominence now given to gender is largely a result of the extension of the word 'sex', so that 'to have sex' has come to mean 'to have sexual intercourse'; 'sex' has become an abstract term for 'sexual activity'.

As we all know, 'love', in English, and 'lust' are easily separable. I loved my grandfather and I love my grandchildren, but in neither case does that cause any sexual excitement. We have, of course, a special use in two phrases: 'to be in love with' or 'to fall in love with', because they are cases in which love and lust are combined and work together. Each of them helps to generate the other.

The Greek vocabulary is rather different. There is one very large set of words from the stem *phil-*, of the kind that you get in *philhellene*, 'lover of the Greeks' or *philately,* 'love of postage stamps'. In one or two occasions in Greek texts, we find that the question 'Do you love me?' can be asked either in a sexual situation or in a parental and familial situation. In the very first scene of Aristophanes' *Clouds*, Strepsiades, the hero or anti-hero of the play, asks his son 'do you love me?', because he is going to try and get his son to do something which his son does not in the least want to do. He uses the verb from the *phil-* stem. This same group of words can be used either of very strong affection at one end of the scale or, indeed, at the other end of the scale in diplomatic contexts where one nation can be described as a 'friend' of another, which does not in itself imply any great access of affection. There is, indeed, one case in a Greek treaty inscribed on stone where the abstract noun *philia* is used to mean simply 'peace' as opposed to 'war'. 'When *philia* has come about', in that particular context means 'when the war is over'. That is a very wide range indeed: it includes sexual love, but it includes every other kind of affection and love and mutual tolerance as well.

In the New Testament, for example in John 3:16, 'for God so loved the world ...', another word is used; the noun is *agape* and the verb *agapan*, which in English translations of the Bible is always translated as 'love'. Students of theology, whose knowl-

80

edge of the pagan world is perhaps not quite as thorough as it might be, came to speak as if *agape* was a Christian invention. One thing that rather precludes that is an early fifth-century vase painting which shows a young lady reclining on a couch (topless and holding a whacking great beaker of wine) and she is named by the painter 'Agape'.

The other set of words which is enormously important are *eros* and the words etymologically connected with *eros*. *Eros* means 'love' in the sense that it has in the English phrases, 'be in love' or 'fall in love'. *Eros* covers quite a range of sexual behaviour, but there is always the sexual element there. The philosopher Prodicus in the fifth century offered a definition. He said that desire doubled (or desire twice over) is *eros*. *Eros* doubled, he added, is insanity. *Eros* is very readily personified, treated as a divine being, as anyone who has walked through Piccadilly Circus will know. What is obscure to us is what exactly the relation is between Aphrodite and Eros. Eros in Greek mythology and poetry is treated as a boy who is a minister or servant or son of Aphrodite, and there were circumstances in which Aphrodite could say to Eros 'Off you go and make A fall in love with B'; Eros shoots A with his arrow and sure enough A does fall in love with B. The point of the arrow symbol is, I think, that we do not choose to fall in love; it is something which happens to us. That is why the Greeks think of it as something coming in from outside.

One could, I suppose, say that, although it would not suit all passages (I'm not sure there is any relationship between Eros and Aphrodite which would suit *all* passages), roughly speaking Aphrodite covers the entire range of sexual activity, whereas Eros covers that species of the genus that involves falling in love and being in love. One interesting thing about Aphrodite is that her sphere covers homosexual as well as heterosexual desire and love. It also covers prostitution. We have quite a number of poems which are dedications by retired prostitutes to Aphrodite, and clearly she is the deity to whom prostitutes look for special protection.

I have seen it suggested, and I think there is something to be said for it, that if Aphrodite is the goddess of anything she could be called with clinical precision the goddess of genital friction. Certainly the Greek term *aphrodisia* is the polite normal term for sexual activity of any kind.

Hippolytus, we are told by Aphrodite in the prologue and we

see for ourselves in the following scene, is immensely hostile to Aphrodite. He is, needless to say, a virgin and evidently he hopes always to remain so. His devotion is to a different goddess, Artemis. Artemis is a rather singular figure in the Greek pantheon. She is essentially the goddess of the wild uncultivated country. Urban situations are alien to her. She is a tireless and relentless hunter, as well as being a champion and protector of the animals of the wild. How exactly the Greeks reconciled being a champion of wild creatures with an absolutely insatiable activity in killing them is hard to say, but perhaps champions of hunting in all ages manage to reconcile the two.

Hunting was a particular activity of young male citizens in fifth-century Athens, and it is entirely in character that Hippolytus should be devoted to hunting. He has a very special affinity, he feels, with Artemis and regards himself as uniquely close to her. He has never seen her. She does not show herself to human devotees, but he does claim actually to have heard her voice, and that is a peculiar and exceptional favour on the part of the goddess. He evidently thinks of wild country, uncultivated country as uniquely pure, and anything associated with it as clean and virtuous.

Now, Aphrodite says in her prologue, 'Well, I don't mind that': he can worship Artemis if he likes, but what Aphrodite does object to is Hippolytus constantly vilifying and insulting her in what he says, and in the lack of any observance that honours her. Greek gods and goddesses are very touchy on this question of honour. What they expect from human beings is a degree of reverence certainly, but also festivals, sacrifices, hymns and so on. If those things are begrudged, then the honour of the god or goddess is offended. Aphrodite finds Hippolytus' slights on her honour intolerable. That is why the events of this play are all part of a design on the part of Aphrodite to punish Hippolytus. Poor Phaedra, of course, is simply the means, the tool, the instrument of that punishment. As we have seen in the prologue, Aphrodite says she is not worried about Phaedra's death.

It is a very general Greek belief that gods and goddesses could cause alterations in people's minds. That is particularly obvious in cases of obvious clinical insanity. But it extends beyond madness in the medical sense to actions, thoughts and behaviour which we could call metaphorically 'mad'. Gods can cause people to behave like that. If people do something which other people feel in their saner or wiser moments they would not have done, then the question arises, 'What god made them behave like this?' Virtually that question occurs in *Oedipus the King*. Towards the end of the play, when Oedipus has blinded himself, the Chorus say to him, 'What deity incited you to do this, to destroy your own eyes?' Rather interestingly, Oedipus draws a distinction. He says that Apollo created the awful situation, but his decision to strike out his eyes was his own. He does not actually blame Apollo for making him do it. Obviously when people behave in an insane way, or in a very rash way which is self-destructive, it *may* be caused by a god, but how can we know?

The idea that self-destructive acts are caused by a god is a general belief which can be held at the same time as one has to admit that in a particular case one cannot know for sure. Since it is not provable that a god distorted one's mind, it does impose a certain limitation on the extent that it can be used as an excuse. If I commit some monstrous crime and say, 'I cannot help it; a god distorted my mind and made me do it', whether I am believed or not depends very much on which side my hearer is on. If you make an excuse like that to friends, they will probably say, 'Yes, yes, of course, it wasn't your fault.' If you make the excuse to enemies – say you are being prosecuted in court or something like that – they may brush it aside and say it is nonsense.

There is a fascinating example in *Iliad* 19, where there has been an awful quarrel between king Agamemnon and Achilles, which has led to so much disaster for the Greek army. In *Iliad* 19 Agamemnon calls the host together and says that his behaviour towards Achilles has been caused by a supernatural force which he calls *ate*, 'destruction' (sometimes 'self-destruction'). He talks about how this dreadful force makes people do what they would not have wished to do. In that particular case, his excuse is accepted because everybody is fed up with the quarrel between Agamemnon and Achilles, and all that is wanted is a face-saving way to end it. Agamemnon achieves this by talking about this external force which affected his mind. This is a case where the circumstances in which the excuse is made are very important. But a hostile hearer can brush aside such an excuse.

There was a play by Euripides called *Cretans*, a lost play of which, however, we do have some bits, including one rather nice extensive bit on papyrus. *Cretans* deals in part with one very bizarre myth, the story of Pasiphae. Pasiphae was the wife of king Minos of Crete. Minos made a vow to Poseidon that if Poseidon sent him an absolutely wonderful bull out of the sea, he would sacrifice it in honour of Poseidon and make a great fuss over the festival. When the bull arrived, Minos decided that he would rather keep it in his own herd, so he sacrificed another bull, which made Poseidon very angry. Poseidon then caused Pasiphae, by this process of divine intervention in the mind, to fall in love with the bull. Plainly consummation of such an affair poses mechanical difficulties, but Pasiphae enlisted the help of Daedalus the great craftsman, who made a hollow wooden cow with cow-hide all round it, which she could get inside. The result of all that was the birth of the monstrous Minotaur which had a bull's head and a human body. Now, we have a bit of this play in which Minos is furious with his wife for behaving in this way, and she makes plain that it was Poseidon, angered by Minos' own action, who inflicted this insanity upon her. But Minos will not listen at all. He simply brushes it aside as if he does not hear what she is saying.

There is a similar case in *Trojan Women*, where Hecuba and Helen are quarrelling after the fall of Troy. Hecuba blames Helen for the disasters which have fallen upon Troy, and Helen says that it was not her fault, because in the famous Judgement of Paris, when the goddesses Aphrodite, Athena and Hera were contending over which was the most beautiful, they asked Paris to judge. All three tried to bribe him. Athena and Hera promised unlimited power; Aphrodite promised him the most beautiful woman in the world. Paris judged that Aphrodite was the winner of the context, and the woman he got was Helen, who happened to be married already to Menelaus. But that didn't matter, so he carried Helen off to Troy (or Helen went with him to Troy), and hence the Trojan War. That is Helen's story, that it wasn't her fault: she was given to Paris by Aphrodite. Hecuba, on the other hand, Priam's widow, the dead Paris' mother, simply says that the whole story of the Judgement of Paris and the contest of the goddesses for beauty is a load of rubbish: it never happened. Helen simply fell for Paris and allowed him to take her off to Troy. This is a case where the accuser does not accept the excuse, simply denies the truth of the story which the defendant is trying to use.

There is another rather interesting passage in *Iliad* 3, where Helen becomes very self-reproachful because of the Trojan War and Priam says to her, 'I don't blame you. It is all the fault of the gods. I hold them responsible for what has happened.' This is sometimes quoted as if it were a universal Greek belief. That, I think, is a mistake, because Priam is always very nice to Helen, he is always very polite to her, he never blames her. His saying, 'I don't blame you, it is all the fault of the gods', is his way of cheering her up when she is full of reproaches against herself.

But whatever the truth of the matter in these other cases may be, here in *Hippolytus* Aphrodite herself in the prologue claims the agency, and Artemis at the end of the play, when she comes in to console the dying Hippolytus, says it was done by Aphrodite. Artemis reproaches Theseus for being too hasty in believing that Hippolytus had actually attempted or succeeded in raping Phaedra, but she forgives Theseus this because, she says, he is only human and when the gods want something to happen, you can't stop it (1433-4). She also says that she will take revenge on Aphrodite by killing some mortal who is a favourite of hers (1420-2). The allusion may be to Adonis, who was indeed a human favourite of Aphrodite, but Artemis says that she will kill this favourite by shooting him with her arrows, and that is not in fact how Adonis in the ordinary version of the myth died. What seems to be happening is that Phaedra and Hippolytus are simply caught up in a feud between Artemis and Aphrodite.

Now, is there any moral issue left in the play? There are plenty of minor issues confined to individual scenes, but we have to remember that when Phaedra falls in love with Hippolytus she does not tell anybody. She keeps silent until it is wrung out of her by her old nurse, and it is the Nurse who actually tries to win Hippolytus over, not Phaedra herself.

It is an interesting thing that this *Hippolytus* that we are going to see is the second play called *Hippolytus* that Euripides wrote. Sophocles also wrote a play called *Phaedra*, about which we know very little. Indeed, we know extremely little about the first *Hippolytus* by Euripides. It has been suggested, not unreasonably, that in the first *Hippolytus* Euripides represented Phaedra not as a victim of Aphrodite and Eros but as taking the initiative herself, and this was not received favourably by the audience, so he wrote another play (the one we have) in which Phaedra does not take the initiative, because she is herself the victim of Aphrodite's anger with Hippolytus. What line Sophocles took in his *Phaedra* we really don't know.

But when all that has been said on Phaedra's behalf, we have to admit that in one very important respect, Phaedra is a monster, because when she learns that Hippolytus has been told by the Nurse about her feeling for him she commits suicide and leaves for Theseus a letter in which she falsely accuses Hippolytus of raping her. That is why Theseus, believing this letter, curses his son. In other words, Phaedra sacrifices Hippolytus' life for the sake of her own reputation. I suppose she couldn't know whether the Nurse would go on and tell anyone else about it, but she couldn't bear the idea of a bad reputation, so she prefers to die. That is very Greek, of course. It is plain from poems about individual deaths and from epitaphs on graves that the Greeks did attach an enormous importance to reputation after death, and Phaedra makes that her top priority.

There is a very interesting contrast there with Hippolytus himself. When the Nurse has told Hippolytus about Phaedra's love for him, he is absolutely outraged and starts raising the roof, and says at once that he will tell his father. But before the Nurse has told him about Phaedra, she has exacted from him an oath that he will never tell anyone about what she is going to say. So when he says that he will tell his father about this, the Nurse reminds him of his oath and he utters a line which became very famous, to the effect that 'my tongue is under oath but my heart is unsworn' (612). The Nurse takes this to mean that it was only words and he did not really mean it. It became a notorious line because the ancients were very bad about taking lines out of context, attributing them to the author of the play as if this was something that he himself believed, and judging him accordingly without any regard for the character or the context or the circumstances in which the line was uttered on stage. Later on in Euripides' life, in the course of a lawsuit that somebody brought against him, his adversary said, 'You couldn't possibly trust the evidence given by a man who had written the line, "my tongue is sworn but my heart is unsworn".'

The interesting thing is that Hippolytus *does* keep his oath. In other words that line, that notorious line, is uttered by him in a moment of anger, but later on when he is accused by his father of having raped his stepmother, which is what Phaedra's untrue letter said, he feels that he cannot break his oath, and so he dies in consequence (1060-3). That makes a rather interesting contrast with Phaedra's outlook on reputation and honour.

As for whether there is any moral lesson in the play as a whole, it has quite often been treated as an illustration of the famous Greek saying 'nothing in excess', in other words: don't go too far in any direction. It has been pointed out that Phaedra is excessively lustful (but we can rule that out, because it has been put in her by Aphrodite), and that Hippolytus is obsessively chaste, and if you are too chaste then trouble will come. Well, will it? I don't know. One thing that we can be pretty sure of is that somebody can be excessively chaste without causing his stepmother to fall in love with him. And the Greek concept of 'nothing in excess' does not, I think, apply to this particular story. Even if Hippolytus were not so obsessively anti-sexual, it is still true that any reasonable young Greek man would feel that it would be a monstrous offence against his father to have any sort of affair with his father's second wife; that is simply a matter of family rules, so to speak. The real moral lesson of the play is: don't give gratuitous offence to a Greek god or goddess; they are not nice people.

ELECTRA

Electra, 1994. Tamsin Shasha as Electra; Alice Kennedy as Clytemnestra.
Photo: daveashtonphotography.com

The date of the first production of Euripides' *Electra* is not known, but was probably between 422 and 413 BC.

aod performed *Electra* in 1994, 1997 and (adapted) 2002.

Guide to mythological detail

The murder of Clytemnestra by Orestes with the help of Electra was a well-known myth. Euripides adheres to the basic outline of the story, but with some divergence in matters of detail. The curse on the House of Atreus produced a cycle of murder and vengeance that spanned several generations. It is not surprising therefore to see in this play some concern with past events.

Distant past

Tantalus was the founder of the dynasty (the sceptre of Tantalus is mentioned in line 11) which suffered more grief than any other house (1176). Neither Tantalus' transgression against the gods, nor his son Pelops' murder of Myrtilus, both considered as origins of the curse on the house, is featured in this play.

Previous generation

In the second choral song (699-746), the Chorus refer to the conflict between the brothers Atreus and Thyestes. Pan presented a golden lamb to the rulers of Argos/Mycenae. Thyestes seized the lamb by seducing Aerope, Atreus' wife, and openly claimed ownership (and therefore power). Zeus changed the course of the sun as a result of this outrage (a lesson for Clytemnestra).

Euripides Talks

Agamemnon and his children

Agamemnon married Clytemnestra, sister of Helen (214) and daughter of Tyndareus, king of Sparta (1018). When Agamemnon (son of Atreus) led the expedition to Troy, the fleet was trapped by contrary winds at Aulis (1022). Agamemnon enticed his daughter Iphigeneia to Aulis on the pretext of marriage to Achilles, but when she arrived he sacrificed her, cutting her throat above the altar (1020-3). After this Agamemnon successfully captured Troy and killed king Priam (5). Aegisthus (son of Thyestes) in contrast stayed at home in Argos (917). On Agamemnon's return, laden with spoils and bringing back the Trojan prophetess Cassandra, he was killed in his own house by his wife Clytemnestra using an axe (160, 1160) and Aegisthus (916) who used a sword (164-5). Agamemnon thus lost the sceptre of Tantalus and Aegisthus is now king (12).

Orestes and Electra were young at the time of their father's murder (284). Orestes was rescued by his old tutor before Aegisthus could kill him. He was raised in Phocis by Strophius (15-18). Electra on the other hand remained in the palace. When she began to attract suitors (one of whom was her uncle Castor, lines 312-13), Aegisthus, afraid that she might bear a noble son to avenge Agamemnon, kept her in the house and would not let her marry (19-24). However, he even feared that she might bear an illegitimate child and made plans to kill her. She was rescued through the intervention of Clytemnestra who felt she had a pretext for killing Agamemnon, but feared resentment if she killed her child (25-30).

Aegisthus put a price on Orestes' head (33) and married Electra off to a peasant of noble lineage whose poverty has eroded his status so that neither he nor any child he might have can pose a threat to Aegisthus (34-42). Electra, when first seen by Orestes is mistaken for a slave since she carries water on her head and her hair is short (suitable for slave or mourner) (107-10). Her peasant husband has not slept with Electra since he is ashamed to take what is beyond his status (43-6). Knowledge of this is kept secret (271) and later in the play Electra will pretend to have given birth.

As the play opens, Orestes has arrived back in Argos secretly with his friend Pylades to avenge the death of his father. At

Agamemnon's grave he has offered tears, a lock of hair and the blood of a black sheep (91-2).

The future

Castor and Polydeuces, brothers of Clytemnestra, appear at the end of the play (as gods who look after ships in storms). Castor reveals that Electra will marry Pylades and Orestes must go to Athens and stand trial on the Hill of Ares for murder. He will be acquitted when votes are equal since Apollo will accept the blame for telling Orestes to carry out the murder (1266-7). Orestes will then found a city in Arcadia. Castor also reveals that only an image of Helen, made by Zeus, went to Troy, while Helen herself spent the time in Egypt. Now she will bury Clytemnestra and the citizens of Argos will bury Aegisthus.

Country matters: the location of Euripides' *Electra*

Chris Carey

The date is some time between 420 and 413. The place is the theatre of Dionysus in Athens, on the southern slope of the Acropolis. The chattering among the audience dwindles as the play is about to begin. Those of us who attended (or had friends who attended) the *Proagon*, the ceremony a few days before the start of the dramatic competitions in which the author appeared with his Chorus and gave a basic advance notice of his plays, will (if our memory holds) have an idea of the cast list and will know the identity of the Chorus as well as the theme of the play. But even those who missed the *Proagon* can make a good guess at what we are about to see. We know the name of the play, *Electra*, and the name conjures up for us a whole range of poetic associations. It also conjures up a legend.

Electra was the daughter of Agamemnon, who led the Greek force in the ten-year siege of Troy. To get to Troy Agamemnon had to sacrifice his daughter Iphigeneia to appease the goddess Artemis, so that the winds which kept his fleet from sailing would drop. Agamemnon paid the price for this sacrifice on his return from Troy, when he was murdered by his wife Clytemnestra. Clytemnestra and her lover Aegisthus were in turn killed by Agamemnon's son Orestes. This story, with variations, had already figured in the Greek epic tradition, and our earliest account, in Homer's *Odyssey*, is so brief and allusive that the story must already have been familiar to his contemporaries, roughly three hundred years before Euripides' play. Orestes' sister Electra had entered the legend at least a couple of centuries before Euripides, and she had assumed a prominent role in avenging the death of her father Agamemnon by at least the first half of the fifth century.

At the very least then we know that we are to see yet another version of the revenge. We can be sure that Orestes and Electra will appear, and probably Clytemnestra and Aegisthus (though it turns out that we are mistaken, at least as far as Aegisthus is concerned). For the rest, we wait to see what Euripides will make of a familiar tale.

The opening is at one level predictable enough. Euripides likes to begin his plays with a set-piece monologue, human or divine, which sets the scene for what follows, placing the action within the legend. True to form, *Electra* opens with 53 lines of narrative from one of the characters. But in fact it is only the monologue form which is predictable. The speaker and what he says send us spiralling away from the familiar landmarks of the legend. This is true in the most literal sense. The other great tragedians of the fifth century whose works survive, Aeschylus and Sophocles, also tell the tale of the avenging of Agamemnon, and both locate the action, as is common in Greek tragedy, in front of the royal palace, at the heart of the city. In Euripides' play, the stage building at the back of the orchestra is not a palace but a rustic house, and we are not in the city of Argos but out in the country. The change is a brilliant theatrical stroke.

The choice of opening speaker reflects another way in which the landmarks of the legend are fundamentally changed by the play. The speaker is not a member of the family of Agamemnon, who belong to the world of the heroes, the world taken over by tragedy from epic. He is a farmer, and not a large landowner but a smallholder, a man who works his own land with his hands. What surprises however is not his status (Euripides' earlier *Medea* for instance had opened with a long speech from Medea's nurse, and Aeschylus' *Agamemnon* forty years earlier opened with a speech from a palace servant) but the novel twist his relationship to the main character gives to the legend. In Aeschylus and Sophocles, Electra remains unmarried, as she must if the killers are to feel safe, and of course as she must if she is to be at home in the palace when Orestes returns from exile to avenge his father (since a married woman will leave her family home to live with her husband). The killers in Euripides are rather more subtle, in that they marry off Electra to someone whose status automatically dictates that of any sons she has and therefore reduces the risk of Electra's offspring becoming the focus of a rebellion. Just as Euripides has evicted us physically from the royal palace, so he has moved the play socially far from the heroic world.

One effect of Euripides' innovation is of course surprise. I've already said something about the tradition behind the play. The legends used by the tragedians were generally familiar to the audience, who grew up with the Greek myths as (say) a genera-tion or two ago people grew up with bible stories. This familiarity could be invaluable for the dramatist. Greek myths were often complex, and no tragedy tells the whole of a saga. The poet selects from the myth a sequence of events to explore. The knowledge of the myth shared by the poet and audience allows the dramatist to rely on the audience working with him, supplying obvious details and responding readily to brief hints which for the modern reader require explanations in printed works. But tradition also makes demands. Themes which have been handled successfully before by different authors, in different media, call for a different kind of originality from what we are used to, the originality of telling an old tale in a way which recaptures its freshness. In actual fact, it is likely that the tragedian saw the tradition not as a burden but as a challenge, an opportunity to put his own stamp on the story. Tragedy in Athens was highly competitive. At one level we have competition between playwrights at the festival, since the performances were judged and ranked. At another we have competition between different versions separated in time, as poets measure themselves against the classic tellings of the past. The Electra theme is not the only one which was handled by all three tragedians. One effect of Euripides' opening, then, is to surprise the audience, to challenge their expectations of the story.

Another effect of Euripides' innovations is enhanced suspense. Where the legend is known to the audience, the basic facts are predictable (for instance, Clytemnestra cannot live, or the legend breaks down), and suspense arises more from the manner of presentation than from major breaks with the story outline. This suspense is increased by the choice of location, which has impli-cations for the stage action. As told by the other two tragedians, the story brings the murderer to the victim. Orestes comes to the palace and must bluff his way in if he is to commit the murders. Euripides' option turns the movement inside out. He has to bring the victim to the killers, and to do so convincingly. His solution is both ingenious and economical. The opening of the play has raised the question of a possible child born to Electra (22-6), and the false news of a birth is plausibly used to entice Clytemnestra out to the country (652-8). It is as though the poet teases the audience by setting a structural problem for himself, with the result that the ingenuity of his solution is all the more impressive. This is Euripides as escape artist.

I have already spoken about competition with successful versions of the past. In the theatre at Athens, this means especially (though not exclusively) competition with the theatrical classics. Here we have a problem. We know that Aeschylus handled the myth in 458. We know that Sophocles wrote an *Electra*. But we do not know the date of Sophocles' play. It is difficult to be sure whether Euripides' play preceded or followed Sophocles'. There is, however, no escaping Euripides' engagement with Aeschylus. Aeschylus' trilogy on the house of Agamemnon had opened with a non-heroic character (though a figure ultimately drawn from epic), the watchman waiting on the roof of the palace for the beacon signalling the fall of Troy. It is difficult not to see in the vivid non-heroic figure who opens *Electra* an attempt to trump the opening of *Agamemnon*. The same process can be seen elsewhere in the play. Aeschylus had brought Orestes face to face with his mother, who showed him her breast, the symbol of motherhood, and urged him not to kill her. Orestes hesitated, but rejected the plea and killed her. In our play the breast motif occurs again, but not as a stage action. Our Orestes too hesitates to kill his mother (962-85). But it is only after the killing that they become fully aware of the horror of what they have done. In a sung exchange Orestes reminds Electra how Clytemnestra exposed her breast (1207) and begged for mercy (1215). This detail both recalls Aeschylus and underlines the different movement of the plot. In Aeschylus the horror of matricide is emphasised both for the audience and for Orestes before he acts. In Euripides the breast motif underlines the wakening of the killers from the mesmeric power of their own desire for vengeance.

The same process of engagement with Aeschylus can be seen shortly after the arrival of the Old Man, in the preparation for the recognition of brother and sister. In Aeschylus' *Libation Bearers* Electra had recognised the presence of her newly returned brother by comparing a lock of hair and footprints at her father's tomb with her own; recognition is assisted by a piece of embroidery which Orestes shows her, made by herself years before. In our play the Old Man has seen offerings (including a lock of hair) at Agamemnon's tomb and he suggests that Orestes may have come back secretly. Electra's response is withering. Different lifestyles make it impossible to compare male and female hair. Well, says the Old Man, try your feet against the footprints at the tomb. Electra replies that the ground is rocky; and anyway, men's feet are bigger. Well, fumbles the Old Man, perhaps your brother would have a garment embroidered by your own hand. Electra remarks that she was a child herself when he was sent away, and such a garment would not fit Orestes now 'unless clothes grow along with the wearer's body' (544). Euripides then goes on to show how a recognition should be managed. He opts for recognition based on a childhood scar, a device taken over from another famous revenge-for-revenge story, the recognition of Odysseus in Homer's *Odyssey*. This is all, as commentators observe, grossly unfair to Aeschylus. It is also very funny. The treatment of Aeschylus is all the more striking for the fact that in the mid-420s his classic status was acknowledged in Athens by a decision that revivals of his plays could be presented at the festivals along with new productions. This is not the only such assault on a theatrical icon in Euripides. His later *Phoenician Women* similarly pokes fun at Aeschylus' *Seven Against Thebes*. As with the changes to the myth announced at the opening, Euripides' approach is flamboyant. But in essence it is the overtness of his competition with past masters which distinguishes him; the practice itself is typical of Greek tragedy.

The mockery of Aeschylus is however more than a piece of fun. The essence of Electra's remarks is that the means of recognition used by Aeschylus were unrealistic, in contrast to Euripides' own approach. Euripides' treatment of heroic legend was controversial, as we know from the comic playwright Aristophanes. In Aristophanes' earliest extant play, *Acharnians*, staged in 425, Euripides is presented as a playwright who habitually brings the heroes of legend into the theatre dressed in rags. Twenty years later Aristophanes included similar criticisms in the debate between the characters Aeschylus and Euripides in his comedy *Frogs*. There Euripides is again accused of presenting heroes in rags, which is seen (by his adversary Aeschylus) as lowering the tone of tragedy, and the character Euripides himself speaks proudly of his introduction of contemporary issues.

Realism is of course a relative thing. In some respects Euripidean tragedy is more stylised that that of his predecessors (particularly at the level of form, for instance, his taste for opening monologues, mocked by Aristophanes, the high fre-

quency of formal debates and of resolutions by a divine appearance at the end of the play). But in content Euripides shows a
marked tendency to reduce the distance between the heroic world
depicted in the acting area and that of the audience sitting in the
auditorium. This is particularly visible in the *Electra*. It can be
seen at the very opening, when instead of a royal palace at the
back of the action we see a humble farmer's house. The role
assigned to the stage building shrinks the heroic world and
creates a more human scale for the action to follow. *Electra* has
a decidedly Odyssean quality. Like Odysseus in Homer, Orestes
returns home in disguise to the edges of his realm and to the
property of one of his subjects. As in the *Odyssey*, the low are as
visible as the high. But more than this, the ruse of marrying
Electra to the farmer puts Electra herself into the subsistence
class. Princes have become peasants. When the Chorus come to
invite her to a festival and she refuses, partly because she hasn't
got a thing to wear (184ff.), they offer to lend her a dress (191ff.).
This is closer to the minutiae of ordinary experience than
Euripides' predecessors. When the farmer invites the disguised
Orestes and his companion into the house, Electra is embar-
rassed at the poor accommodation, and the farmer himself notes
that he has just about enough to entertain for a day. There is
however nothing casual about the process. In reducing the drama
to human proportions Euripides diminishes distance, the distance between enactment and observer, and proportionately
increases the relevance of the emotions and experiences of the
characters to the audience. In a play like this, the divine intervention at the close is all the more important, since one of its
effects is to fit the action we have witnessed back into the legend
we know.

This narrowing of distance can be seen in some aspects of
characterisation. The Orestes of Aeschylus and Sophocles comes
boldly to the city to confront his victims. Our Orestes has only to
come into the outlying countryside and even so he is ready for a
quick getaway if need be (96-7). His realistic caution is pointed
up by the rather romantic notion Electra has of her brother. She
cannot imagine that he would come furtively (525-6). And when
the time for planning comes, Orestes is no leader but is guided by
Electra and the Old Man. Electra herself is also no lofty heroine.
So far from being a paradigm of endurance under suffering, as
she appears in Sophocles, she comes across as revelling in her

misery to an unnecessary degree, though her characterisation is not entirely negative, since she shows loyalty and affection for the farmer. Her hostility to Clytemnestra seems to owe as much to an envy of Clytemnestra's possessions as a concern to see justice done.

If the avengers appear to be less than admirable characters, the murderers they kill also emerge as rather ambiguous figures. As early as the farmer's opening speech we learn that Aegisthus had intended to kill Electra but that Clytemnestra had intervened to save her daughter. When she comes to visit Electra, one strand at least of her emotions appears to be maternal concern. She is both distressed at the state to which Electra has been reduced and conciliatory in the debate with her daughter. Aegisthus does not appear in person in the play, but his murder by Orestes is narrated in a messenger speech. In neither Sophocles nor Aeschylus does Aegisthus' murder inspire any complicated emotions. Unlike the killing of Clytemnestra, which is matricide, the killing of Aegisthus is simply justified revenge, and he is given no redeeming features which might complicate our response to his death. In Euripides' play he is given (in the account of his welcome to Orestes when Orestes turns up at the sacrifice) a certain bluff good humour, and his killing is complicated both by our awareness that Orestes is his guest when he kills him, and that the killing takes place at a sacrifice (though technically Orestes contrives to avoid impiety by refusing to share in the ritual cleansing before the sacrifice), and by the lingering nature of his death (which is not recounted in Sophocles and Aeschylus). This presentation, in which neither the avengers nor their victims are morally uncomplicated, brings home the horror of revenge, a reaction which is given further impetus by the revulsion of Electra and Orestes after the event and by the judgement of Castor and Pollux on Apollo's role in ordering the revenge, when they enter to terminate the play (1245-6).

Related to the change in the proportions of the heroic world is the introduction of contemporary ideas. As I have mentioned, this is a feature claimed for Euripidean tragedy in Aristophanes' *Frogs*. It is quite common for characters in Euripides to conduct their debates in the terminology, and using the ideas, of their fifth-century contemporaries. One of the issues debated in the fifth century was the relationship between virtue, birth and teaching. *Arete*, excellence, had always been claimed by the aris-

tocrats as their own prerogative. But the emergence of the sophists, the itinerant teachers who provided higher education to
those who could afford it, in the fifth century carried, with their
claim that they could teach a man to run his own and the city's
affairs better, the suggestion that excellence is merely an intellectual capacity which can be acquired. The idea that rich and
poor, well-born and base, might be closer to each other than
tradition supposed was also fostered by a political system (the
radical democracy) which, while it effectively gave political initiative to the wealthy, nonetheless gave the final say in all political
affairs to the mass of ordinary citizens.

These issues are brought to the fore by the location of the
drama and the prominence (early in the play at least) of the
farmer. The choice of a peasant was not accidental. Nowadays, if
we wanted to show a character who was poor but honest we would
probably go for someone working on an assembly line or in the
service sector. For the Greeks, financial independence was an
important ideal, and this is reflected by the evaluation of paid
work by Athenian writers, and not only philosophers. The man
who farms his own land is his own man, unlike the craftsman, the
market trader or the hired labourer. It is no accident than a
decade or more later (in *Orestes*), when Euripides wanted to
contrast the simple decent man with the unscrupulous politician
in the debate at the assembly at Argos, he returned to the
peasant farmer as an ideal. Thus for Euripides the character of
the farmer came loaded with ideological implications. Here is a
man living at subsistence level who, offered a princess to share
his bed, respects her status. His nobility is pointed up by the
cynicism of Orestes' response when he first hears that the farmer
has not had sex with his wife, which attributes the farmer's
restraint to base motives, arrogance, vanity, fear (254ff.). The
farmer is sensitive to questions of honour and shame (as he
proves when he is suspicious of the strangers talking to his wife,
in a culture where decent women do not talk to male outsiders).
He is a zealous host and is loyal to the dispossessed royal family.
The farmer's generous hospitality (as generous as his poverty will
permit) prompts from Orestes a lengthy comment on the paradox
which finds such nobility of spirit in one so poor (377ff.). The
comments ironically point up Orestes' own behaviour. By this
time he knows the farmer to be loyal; but he continues to conceal
his identity. The peasant's simple and consistent morality is a

101

yardstick against which to measure the lack of frankness in the prince. The questions of true nobility and of wealth and poverty are also raised by the farmer himself. When Electra criticises him for inviting nobles into his house, he responds that if the visitors are truly noble they will tolerate a little privation (406-7). And before setting off to fetch the Old Man he observes that once one's basic needs are satisfied, the poor are no worse off than the rich (430-1). When the Old Man enters, Orestes asks (553-4): 'Electra, to whom does this ancient relic of humanity belong?' This is the same Orestes who earlier, when confronted with the nobility of the peasant, reflected on the gap between appearance and reality, social status and inner worth. When prince and peasant are measured together, in this play the prince does not necessarily emerge as superior.

The location of the play (physically and socially) proves then to be loaded with potential, for surprise, for suspense and for the ethical orientation both of the characters and of the play as a whole.

Hope deferred makes the heart sick: Euripides'*Electra*

Jasper Griffin

The story of king Agamemnon is one of the most important of all Greek myths. The great king of Mycenae led a coalition from all Greece against the city of Troy; he took Troy, the supreme achievement of Greek heroism; on his return home he was murdered by the lover of his unfaithful wife; and in the end his murder was avenged by his son Orestes, who slew cowardly Aegisthus, the killer of his father. So needful is it to have a son; and to be a good son.

That is the form in which the story comes in the *Odyssey*, in which it is repeatedly held up as an example to another son of a hero returning from the Trojan War: Telemachus, son of Odysseus. He, too, might have found himself in the position of Orestes, if his mother Penelope had yielded to one of the Suitors and broken her ties to husband and son. And, among other things, the story embodies the perennial anxiety of the fighting man, away from home on campaign: What is going on back home? And specifically: How is my wife behaving? There are always men snooping about, bad types who kept out of the army, trying to seduce our wives. In mythical terms, the two wives, Penelope and Clytemnestra, represent the two possibilities, loyalty or betrayal.

It will be seen that this story is different in important respects from what we find in the Attic tragedians. First, it is Aegisthus, the lover of Clytemnestra, who kills the king; not the unfaithful wife herself. Second, we are never told in the *Odyssey* how Clytemnestra died. The nearest we come to the matricide that so fascinated the tragic poets is the statement in Book 3 that Orestes slew Aegisthus: 'and when he had celebrated the funeral games of his hateful mother and of cowardly Aegisthus ...'. That strongly suggests that the poet (some call him Homer) was indeed familiar with the story of the matricide, but that he preferred to suppress it. That would be in line with other suppressions in the Homeric poems, such as that of the sacrifice of Agamemnon's daughter Iphigeneia: another story which there is reason to believe that Homer deliberately cut out. The ethos of the Homeric poems, utterly different from that of tragedy, involves reducing to a minimum, or suppressing altogether, the horrid, the creepy, and the morally messy: human sacrifice, incest, cannibalism, killing within the family.

Thirdly, it is of special interest to us to note, there is no acknowledgement in Homer of the existence, much less of a role in the drama of matricide, for Agamemnon's daughter, Electra. The great king had in fact three daughters, we hear in *Iliad* 9: their names are those of the virtues of a king – Golden Justice (Chrysothemis), Equity for the People (Laodice), and Ruler by Might (Iphianassa). Clearly Iphianassa excludes Iphigeneia: both names cannot co-exist in the same set of siblings, and in the tenth year of the Trojan War Iphianassa is still alive. And as three is the right number of daughters for a myth or fairy story – think of King Lear, and Cinderella, and Psyche and her two sisters – we can be pretty sure that what Homer gives us is meant as an exhaustive list of Agamemnon's daughters.

Attic tragedy homes in on just those aspects of the myth that the epic avoids. It is the sacrifice by Agamemnon of his own daughter Iphigeneia, and the killing of Clytemnestra by her own son Orestes, that fascinates the tragic poets. You see how the story is turned from an up-beat one, of the avenging of a crime by a good son, to a dubious and horrid one. The act of matricide is ghastly: and Agamemnon's own hands were far from clean.

As usual, we cannot start to understand our play without looking briefly at its fore-runners and the position in which Euripides found himself when he started to compose it. The great tragic poet of the last generation, Aeschylus, in his *Oresteia*, transformed the character and the atmosphere of the tale. We can list the main changes as follows:

(i) It was Clytemnestra who killed Agamemnon. This is a much more sinister and upsetting affair. Every man, however powerful or astute, must at times be helpless in the presence of his wife. She produces his food, and his clothes; we remember Herakles, killed when his wife put on him a garment that she had poisoned. She sees him asleep; and of the 50 daughters of Danaus, we recall, 49 cut the throats of their bridegrooms in the course of the first night. She may see him in the bath; and it is there, where a man feels safest, that Agamemnon was killed, when his wife came towards him, not with a towel but with a sword. Aeschylus develops the motif more generally, to a creepy pattern of sex reversal: Clytemnestra is a manly woman, Aegisthus an effeminate man. Nature itself is being defiled.

(ii) Orestes kills not only his enemy Aegisthus but also his mother; the climax of the story is not the killing of Aegisthus but that of Clytemnestra.

(iii) These family killings form a pattern through the generations. Agamemnon's father had killed the children of his own brother Thyestes and served their flesh to their father in a cannibal feast; Agamemnon sacrificed his daughter Iphigeneia; Clytemnestra killed her husband Agamemnon; Orestes killed his mother Clytemnestra; and the sack of Troy is to be seen in the same perspective, as it involved the slaughter of the innocent children – and that is why Agamemnon had to sacrifice his own child.

(iv) There is a role for Agamemnon's daughter Electra. She has suffered from the usurpation of Aegisthus and Clytemnestra, and she has an affecting scene of recognition with her brother Orestes – evidently they had been long apart – after which she joins her voice with his at Agamemnon's grave, praying to the powers of the dead for vengeance: a great musical scene. [But before the actual killing she disappears.]

(v) Orestes is [but Electra is not] hounded by the Furies for the matricide; finally acquitted in Athens.

In the next generation both Sophocles and Euripides, in their handling of the myth:

(i) omit *both* the climactic scene of the mother pleading for her life; *and* the big musical scene at Agamemnon's grave. Clearly these celebrated scenes, unforgettably written by Aeschylus, cannot be done over again.

(ii) see Electra as the area for development: her emotions and reactions.

Sophocles sets about this by

(a) giving Electra a sister, Chrysothemis, who by being an ordinary girl contrasts with, and brings out, the extraordinariness of Electra. This is a favourite Sophoclean technique, as we see from Antigone's sister Ismene, and indeed from the untragic and essentially ordinary Creon who contrasts with Oedipus in *Oedipus the King*; and

(b) by the ingenious idea (*sophisma*) of developing the ruse of Orestes, who in Aeschylus gains access to the palace by announcing Orestes' death, so that it is believed by Electra, too. This gives scope for full and highly pathetic development of her character and emotions: especially the celebrated scene of Electra weeping over the urn which she believes to contain the ashes of her brother.

Euripides has a *sophisma* of a very different kind. It is as if he had asked himself: What would Aegisthus *really* have done about the irreconcilable daughter Electra? Instead of keeping her in the palace, threatening her with a dungeon if she does not stop denouncing him, and so on: what a good idea it would be, to marry her off to some non-noble person! Thus she is got off the scene, away in the hills; and she is rendered harmless, *déclassé*, and the future mother of offspring who will be outside the heroic class and so incapable of revenge (268).

We are to think of this as a deft solution; frustrated, indeed, by the unexpected and almost incredible virtue of the husband (258-61), who does not take advantage of his position and exercise his conjugal rights (43-4), but Aegisthus is not to know that. It also is pre-eminently unheroic. Electra is to be silenced by being made socially misplaced. We are told that Aegisthus makes a practice of getting drunk and throwing stones and hurling taunts at Agamemnon's grave (326ff.). He is altogether a low character, not even a great villain: someone who does not belong in the grand company of the heroic myths. And the position of Electra is unbearable, not for reasons of physical sufferings or threats, which could at least be in the grand manner, but because of social resentment and social *déplacement*.

Electra has been in this painful position for a long time: she was young, we hear, when she lost her brother (284), and so she does not recognise him. Euripides makes the motif of 'long separation', which in Aeschylus was not made explicit, effective and central to his play. Orestes is in exile, sending messages but not coming in person. Meanwhile, her long wait has had an effect on Electra. She is seen at the beginning of the play fetching water from the well, not because she really has to but to show her miserable plight; her husband urges her to stop, but she insists (64ff.). We all, I think, are familiar with that sort of ostentatious self-martyrdom. When she says to her husband 'Orestes has sent these men to observe my woes', he replies, dryly, 'Some part they can see, and I suppose you are telling them the rest' (355). She is in rags, as she insistently tells us. She is obsessed with the falseness of her position: she can mix freely neither in the company of unmarried girls nor in that of married women, as she is not really married (311ff.). The women of the Chorus invite her to a dance; No, she has nothing to wear (167ff.). They offer to lend her some ornaments for the occasion, but again, No, she refuses (190ff.). She snubs her husband when he invites the disguised Orestes and Pylades into his house: 'They are too grand for you!' (404-5).

It is appropriate to the story that Electra should be irreconcilable in her hatred of her mother and her paramour; but in this play it is made very clear that a powerful element in her feelings is resentment about her social and economic come-down. 'Look at my clothes', she says, 'and look how dirty I am, and what sort of house I live in, after the royal palace' (304ff.). She has to make her own clothes, 'or else I shall be naked and have nothing' (307f.). Meanwhile, her mother 'sits on a throne wearing the loot of Phrygia', surrounded by the maid-servants 'whom my father won, all wearing dresses of Eastern luxury and gold brooches' (314ff.). When her mother comes to her house, Electra offers to help her out of her carriage, saying, 'Let me take your blessed hand, since I am a servant, ejected from my father's house and living in poverty' (1004ff.). 'There are servants to do that, please don't exert yourself', replies Clytemnestra. As her mother walks in to her death, the last words that Electra throws at her retreating back are the sarcastic taunt, 'Enter my impoverished house; and please be careful my smoky walls don't dirty your clothes' (1139f.). These hoarded resentments, we feel, underlie the violence with which she says to Orestes, 'Yes, I am prepared to kill my mother, and with the same weapon with which she killed my father', and then bursts out. 'Let me die, when I have shed my mother's blood!' (278-81).

She is passionate in her demands of Orestes. His friendship is not worth much, while he is far away (245); it is high time he was here! (275). Even as an exile, it will be a disgrace if he can't kill one man, Aegisthus: he is better born, after all (336ff.). Orestes, who in exile has learnt to trust nobody, does not live up to his sister's fantasies about him. 'My brave brother would not enter the country in disguise for fear of Aegisthus', she says (524ff.), in the presence of her disguised brother; who does not, even then, declare himself, but who has to be unmasked by the old retainer who remembers him from long ago. 'You must be a man,' she tells Orestes, who betrays little enthusiasm for the task, even before he goes off to kill Aegisthus (693); before tackling his mother he has definite scruples, which Electra beats down (969-85): 'Don't be a coward!' she taunts him (982).

It is worth looking at the way in which usurper and murderess are killed. In the case of Aegisthus, Orestes comes up to him as he is performing a sacrifice; courteously invited to take part, and given the sacrificial axe, he strikes Aegisthus in the back with it as he is examining the entrails of the sacrificial victim. As for Clytemnestra, she is entangled in the clever scheme by which Electra has supposedly been neutralised. Electra pretends that she really has given birth to a child – the unroyal, unmenacing child – for which she was married off, and her mother comes, as a real mother would, to assist her daughter in this moment of need. That is how she is got away from her guards and protection; and so she is killed. Aegisthus is cut down in a religious cere-mony; Clytemnestra is ambushed and killed as she attends the childbed of her daughter, not before she has said, half apologeti-cally, 'I am not so very pleased, my child, with my actions' (1105f.). The episodes are both rather ugly, the former close to sacrilege, and the latter taking ruthless advantage of Clytemnes-tra's better and more human impulses.

The matricide is immediately followed by a violent revulsion of feeling and collapse on the part of both brother and sister. 'It's my fault!' cries Electra (1183); and the Chorus reply that now she is in the right, when before she was in the wrong; 'And what you have done to your brother, who didn't want to, terrible' (1201ff.). Castor and Polydeuces, appearing on the machine to end the play, criticise the oracle of Apollo that drove the pair to matricide, and they announce the separate destinies that will keep Orestes and Electra apart. The play closes with the brother and sister, so recently re-united, going sadly and separately off.

Euripides has transformed the old tale, and produced an up-to-date, interesting play for the second half of the fifth century, with two strokes of invention: first by his invention of Electra's pseudo-marriage; and second by unpacking the idea of Orestes' long absence and spelling out its consequences. In the plays of Aeschylus and Sophocles time has passed, but it has not really affected the characters of brother and sister; in Euripides' tragedy, we see with painful clarity the effect of long disappointment on Electra, and of long concealment on Orestes. And that, too, is tragic.

TROJAN WOMEN

Trojan Women, 1996. Tamsin Shasha as Helen;
Maria Fierheller as Hecuba; Mark Katz as Menelaus.
Photo: Simon Warner

✂

The play was first performed as part of a trilogy, followed by a satyr play at the City Dionysia in the spring of 415 BC.

Trojan Women has proved to be one of **aod**'s most successful adaptations, touring in 2002, 2004 and 2005. They first performed it in translation in 1996.

Guide to mythological detail

Set in the immediate aftermath of the destruction of Troy, it contains numerous references to events past and events to come.

Geography

Mount Ida is a major feature of the mythical landscape of Troy. Through the plain of Troy flow two rivers, the Scamander and its smaller tributary the Simois which joins the Scamander just before it flows into the Hellespont.

The distant past

Dardanus, son of Zeus (1288), was one of the earliest kings of the region. His grandson Tros gave his name to Troy.

Laomedon, grandson of Tros, had the walls of Troy built by Apollo and Poseidon (4-5). When Laomedon refused payment for their services, Poseidon sent a sea monster to which the Trojans offered Hesione, Laomedon's daughter. Herakles offered to kill the monster on condition that Laomedon gave him some horses, a gift of Zeus. But after he rescued Hesione, Laomedon refused to hand over the promised horses (809-10). As a result Herakles led an expedition against Troy. Telamon, king of Salamis, was among the Greeks who accompanied Herakles (799ff.). Laomedon was killed, the walls destroyed and the city sacked (812-6).

Among Laomedon's children were Hesione, Priam, Ganymede and Tithonus.

Ganymede (822), was carried off by Zeus to be his cup-bearer on Olympus. Tithonus was carried off by Eos (Dawn) to be her husband (847-57).

The recent past: the reign of Priam

The story of Paris and Helen (mostly as told by Helen 919-65)

The youngest son of Priam and Hecuba is called Paris or Alexander. Hecuba dreamed that she gave birth to a firebrand which set fire to Troy (922). This was interpreted as an omen that Paris would bring destruction on Troy. Instead of having the child killed, they exposed Paris on Mount Ida where he was brought up by shepherds.

When the goddess Eris (Discord) threw the golden apple (inscribed 'to the fairest') into the company of gods at the wedding of Peleus and Thetis, the three claimants were sent by Zeus to Paris for judgement. Athena offered Paris the conquest of Greece, Hera offered power over Asia and Europe, and Aphrodite offered Helen (924-31; Hecuba pours scorn on the story 970ff.). Paris' choice brought about the destruction foretold before his birth.

While Paris was visiting Sparta, Menelaus sailed to Crete, leaving Helen behind. Paris carried her off from Sparta, despite the presence of her brothers Castor and Polydeuces/ Pollux (1000-1) who were later immortalised (the constellation Gemini). The Greeks came to get Helen back (130), although Agamemnon had to sacrifice his daughter Iphigeneia to placate Artemis before they could sail (370-3). There ensued a ten-year war (20) during which Hector, Troy's greatest warrior, was killed (394ff.).

When Paris was killed, Helen tried to escape from Troy (she claims in 955-8), but was then married to Deiphobus despite opposition from the Trojans (959-60).

The Sack of Troy

The Greeks finally took Troy by the ruse of the wooden horse (9-14, 515ff.). Priam has been killed at the altar of Zeus (16-17, 482-3). Ajax, son of Oileus, has outraged Athena by dragging Cassandra by force from her temple (69-70). Polyxena has been sacrificed at the tomb of Achilles (39-40, 260-71, 622-9), and now, as the play begins, the women of Troy are waiting to be allocated to their new Greek masters.

The future

Athena and Poseidon will wreck the Greek fleet on its voyage home (77-97). Cassandra gives a detailed description of Odysseus' travels on his homeward voyage (427-43) and says that Hecuba will die at Troy, giving only a vague hint of the story of Hecuba's metamorphosis into a bitch (430). Cassandra has been allocated to Agamemnon and she foresees both his death and her own, and the ensuing matricide when Orestes avenges the death of his father (356-64, 444-50).

Trojan Women: sex and the city

Carmel McCallum-Barry

Trojan Women is an unsettling play in many ways. Its episodic construction presents us with a succession of scenes, each serving to add more misery to the previous ones, so it has no plot in any complex sense, no denouement of the action such as we see in other tragedies. It is unsettling because it is hard to say what the play is 'about' when there is such a variety of subject matter and themes to focus on. We could say that it is about war and its aftermath, for it is immediately obvious that we are concerned with the suffering of the victims of war. Euripides makes it clear that the conquerors will suffer too, as the victorious Greeks are guilty of behaviour that will soon bring them misfortune. Such a reversal of fortune fits well with themes of the instability of fortune for humankind and the uncertainty of divine favour, which recur throughout the play. The other important issue that keeps coming up for consideration is that of responsibility; who is to blame for the disasters that have happened and those that are still to come? The most forcible statements from both Trojans and Greeks insist that Helen is the guilty one, responsible for everything.

The diversity of issues explored in the play means that we must look for some larger topic that the play is 'about', one that can include all the rest. I suggest we say that *Trojan Women* is about the annihilation of a city, and for Greeks, who could not consider a full life possible except as members of a city-state, it is an almost apocalyptic vision of the end of a world. The world is a man's world but it is examined through women's suffering; as so often in Euripides' plays, problematic issues concerning the city are explored through female characters. The technique is poignantly apt in this play. The women are representative of the sphere of family and personal relationships which underpin any society. When these relationships are expressed in regulated marriage (or 'good Eros', as choruses in drama frequently call it) they are vital to the patriarchal city-state; harmonious and fruitful unions produce new citizens and promote the city's growth and prosperity. In *Trojan Women* it is unhappily clear that marriages or erotic unions in the wider sense are implicated in the city's destruction, no union mentioned in the play has a happy ending. So we have two aspects of social breakdown, state and personal, which constantly interact.

If we consider the play as a tale of the city's destruction the subjects and themes dealt with fit into a tightly constructed pattern; war, suffering, unfortunate marriages, the uncertainty of fortune and the issue of responsibility all form part of the overarching story of the death of Troy. Looking from this point of view we see more clearly that the city has been guilty and is responsible for its own destruction; in the personal sphere it becomes apparent that each disaster mentioned can be linked with a marriage or erotic union. This means of course that the status of the city and of Hecuba as innocent victims is seriously undermined; in Euripides, being a victim is no guarantee of innocence. It also means that we should look more closely at Hecuba, since she is the surviving member of the Trojan royal family, whose destiny can be equated with that of the city. In fact during the course of the play it becomes clear that the guilt of Troy is principally the guilt of its ruling family.

Hecuba was once queen of Troy and now in *Trojan Women* is a symbol of the fallen city; her role is twofold since she is the city but is also one of the women of the title, her griefs stand for theirs. Her identification with Troy is underlined by the language of the play; she lies on the ground as Troy lies in ruins, she falls, trembles and totters as does the city; when the city is set on fire she tries to rush into the flames to become one with it. She exemplifies the pride and wealth of the great city in constantly asserting her once lofty state. As one of the women she will soon, like them, cease to exist as a Trojan, because as well as the destruction of the material remains of the city we are also confronted with the destruction of all its inhabitants, either physically (the male warriors), or by displacement, since the women and children lose their identity when carried off to foreign lands as slaves.

The episodes of the play are linked in the first place by Hecuba's physical presence, but also by the theme of Eros; each successive scene between the individual women and Hecuba presents the subject of unfortunate marriage from a different

117

perspective. Meanwhile the linked choral odes reflect on the ruined life of the ordinary women of Troy and on the problematic unions of the Trojan royal family in the past as well as its culpability on the larger historical canvas.

In the Prologue, Poseidon, hitherto patron of the Trojans, and Athena, supporter of the Greek conquerors, set the scene. Poseidon tells of the defeat of Troy; the streets and holy places run with blood, all the men are dead, king Priam himself has been butchered at the altar of Zeus. The Greeks are now preparing to sail home with their booty which includes the women now waiting to be assigned to their new masters. It is interesting to see that Spartan Helen is considered a Trojan woman and, Poseidon says, is rightly classed among the prisoners. He directs our attention to the aged Hecuba lying on the ground; her husband and sons are dead, one daughter Polyxena has just been sacrificed at the tomb of Achilles and another is a living source of grief. This is Cassandra who is a prophet, intended to remain virgin in the service of the gods, and Apollo has made her into a frenzied prophet because she rejected his advances. She too is one of the prisoners and Agamemnon, leader of the Greeks 'will marry her by force' (44), casting aside respect for things divine. Athena enters and shifts focus to the conquerors. She is withdrawing her support from them and wants Poseidon to help in 'bringing pleasure to the Trojans and giving the Greeks an unhappy return home' (65-6). Athena is deserting the Greeks because their leaders did not punish impious offences committed against her in Troy when her temple was violated and the priestess Cassandra forcibly dragged off (raped?). Poseidon agrees to help, for 'the man who sacks cities and temples is a fool – he himself perishes later' (95-7).

The Prologue not only gives us background information, it gives us background mood too, a predisposition to feel pity for the suffering women and a willingness to think that the Greeks will get their just deserts. The exchange between the gods is programmatic too, for here at the beginning they demonstrate the interaction between the divine level of activity and the human, both in its collective form as the city and in the individuals who make up the city. Not only has Athena been insulted by the Greeks but Zeus the king of gods has seen the king of Troy cut down at his altar. The uncertainty of divine favour is also made obvious before any human has a chance to complain of it.

After the gods have finished 'setting' the play from a divine perspective, Hecuba does much the same thing from the Trojan point of view. In her opening song she twice refers to her family's former pride and wealth, her former royal status as queen and leader of the women of Troy. She uses imagery connected with ships and sailing to tell herself she must go with the current, not try to sail against the wind. This imagery, which recurs throughout the play, is always ominous.

The Chorus of women who enter echo Hecuba's misery and extend the sailing motif to lead into the following scene. The Greeks are ready to sail home, soon the women will learn which chief will be their new master. They lament, not lost royal status but loss of the female routines of ordinary marriage in their native land. No longer will they weave at Trojan looms, carry water from Trojan fountains or see their parents' homes, they mourn for life at home with loved ones, while Hecuba mourns for the pomp of state.

The Greek herald next announces the individual fates of the women of the royal family: Hecuba's daughter Cassandra will have the good fortune to go to the bed of Agamemnon, the other daughter Polyxena, he says enigmatically, will serve the tomb of the dead hero Achilles. Andromache, her daughter-in-law, widow of Hector, will be taken by the son of Achilles and Hecuba herself will be a slave to Odysseus. The news arouses strong reaction from Hecuba for herself, she cries out against having to serve this treacherous man, a master of double talk, twister of words. The first scene between Hecuba and the individual women follows immediately as flames and smoke are seen and the frenzied Cassandra rushes on waving torches as if for a marriage ceremony. She sings a song of joy for her coming union with Agamemnon, even asks her horrified mother to dance with her. Though Hecuba and the other women are appalled and distressed, the significance of this marriage is clear to Cassandra and to us. It means the death of Agamemnon and the ruin of his family – in fact, the Greeks are less fortunate than the Trojans! Her reasons for this crazy statement make sense within the overall ideology of the play, for they spring from the intimate, family point of view. While besieging Troy, the Greeks could not see their wives and families, they died away from home, denied burial at the hands of their loved ones; the Greek leader actually killed a beloved child in order to go to Troy.

The Greek herald perceives the threatening nature of Cassandra's prophecy and hurries her off, but Hecuba cannot accept Cassandra's ravings as true, and in a speech (466-510) reverts to her own previous proud fortunes. She was born from and married into the ruling family, she produced superior children, but the males are now dead, the girls who were prepared for the best of marriages are now ruined and she, the mother of Hector, now lies as a slave on the floor instead of on a royal bed. It is easy to listen to this story of past grandeur and present misery and feel pity, but we should also listen to the notes of arrogance and excessive pride in the background. Hecuba is Troy in this play, and it is a commonplace in Greek literature that the legendary wealth and pride of Troy led to the city's downfall. The women of the Chorus once again take a wider view and in their first ode tell how the blind folly of the Trojans led them to joyous celebrations as they brought the fateful Horse into the city; the recurrent motifs of the play form part of the tale. The Horse was hauled along with ropes like a ship, the celebrations were lit with fiery torches, in the disaster that followed mothers and children were terrified, men slain at altars, and the young women, with no hope of rightful marriage, became a prize of victory for the conquerors, destined to produce children for Greeks, not Trojans. The Chorus treat the same themes as Hecuba does but reflect on the fate of the city as a whole rather than on that of the royal family as the city.

Their reflections lead naturally into the next episode and the entry of Andromache, carrying her child, the son of Hector; she is being taken off to serve the bed of Achilles' son. She brings Hecuba news of fresh misery, that Polyxena has been sacrificed as a gift to the dead Achilles. This princess of Troy, prepared by her mother for a noble marriage, has become the bride of death, as will Cassandra. Andromache, however, feels that Polyxena is fortunate to be dead, and speaks of her own fortunes in marriage. She was a model wife to Hector, behaved properly in every way, her reward now is that her high reputation has made her desirable to the son of the man who killed her husband. 'I shall be a slave in the house of murderers' (660). Her dilemma is serious, if she goes willingly to the bed of her new master she will be a traitor to Hector's memory; on the other hand if she does not go willingly she will be hated by her master. It is equally serious for the issues of the play, as whatever she does will involve betrayal of one of the marriages. She concludes that death is preferable to her situation. Hecuba's response is startling, she begins thoughts of sailing on a sea of troubles, then advises Andromache to stop mourning Hector and honour her new husband, advice which seems callous and at variance with her character as established so far. But it is consistent with what she has already said in 'sea of troubles' vein and it echoes her previous resolve to go with the currents, because the course she recommends is a way for Troy to survive. If Andromache can co-exist with Achilles' son she can bring up her own and Hector's child in safety. The child's name, Astyanax, means 'lord of the city'; like Hecabe he is a symbol of Troy, so his survival can mean survival of the city.

However, as we might expect, such hopes are doomed, and immediately the herald announces that the Greeks have no intention of allowing a male of the Trojan royal family to survive; Astyanax is to be killed by being thrown from the walls of Troy. Andromache's marriage is revealed after all as a tragic one, 'a bed and marriage unfortunate' (745), 'a fine marriage I am going to, when I have lost my child' (778-9) she says. The Chorus pick up the thought, Troy has lost all her children for the sake of one woman (Helen) and her hateful marriage; once more the city and its continued life are linked to the quality of marriage.

In the following ode (799-859) the Chorus goes back in time and probes earlier episodes in Trojan history. It is often said that the content intensifies the sympathy we feel for Troy, but I think not. On the contrary, it demonstrates once again that Troy and its royal family are in no small way deserving of blame, and that in the past too unfortunate erotic unions played a part in disaster for Troy. In the ode's complex mythological frame of reference, events actually narrated and others that are inferred reveal Troy and its royal family as doomed and culpable in the previous generation. The story, according to the Chorus, is that Herakles rescued the daughter of king Laomedon (Priam's father) from a sea monster, and as a reward Laomedon had promised to give the hero mares of a breed given to him by Zeus. But Laomedon cheated the hero of his reward so Herakles led an expedition against Troy and sacked the city. There is no judgement made, but a parallel can be drawn with the present situation. What is not mentioned in the ode, but all would know, is that Laomedon made a habit of faithlessness. He had even reneged on his agreement with the gods Apollo and Poseidon by refusing to pay them for helping to build the walls of Troy.

The Chorus continues with a reference to Laomedon's son Ganymede who was loved by Zeus and taken to be his cupbearer on Olympus. It appears that the Trojans expected some special treatment from the gods because of Ganymede's favour on Olympus, but in vain, 'you beside the throne of Zeus keep your face beautiful in its calm' (835-7). This love affair is the only non-problematic union mentioned in the play; the reason perhaps is simply that both Zeus and Ganymede are totally detached, uninvolved in Trojan woes. One other amorous relationship linking Troy and its royal family with the gods is alluded to briefly, but significantly in a section beginning with an invocation to Eros, Eros who came from the gods and made Troy great. The love referred to is that of the goddess of the Dawn for Tithonus, another son of Laomedon, whom she persuaded Zeus to make immortal. The union brought no benefit to Troy and only flawed happiness for Tithonus, for according to other versions of the myth, he was not given immortal youth, and the goddess grew tired of her ageing lover. The last line of this ode sums up everything for Troy, 'the charms of love with the gods are gone' (858-9).

This choral ode encapsulates present as well as past problems of Troy. These problems clearly derive from the royal family which was loved by the gods in the past, but treachery on the part of humans led to the destruction of the city itself. This fatal combination is strongly marked as the real dynamic of the play by its reappearance in the following dramatic episode. The same associations of Trojans, gods, Eros/marriage and betrayal form the subject of debate when Helen is brought to face Hecuba and Menelaus, the husband she abandoned to go with Paris to Troy. Menelaus insists that he came to Troy, not so much to get back Helen, as for revenge on Paris who had betrayed the code of hospitality when he was a guest of Menelaus' in Sparta. The Trojans now have paid the price for this treachery; as for Helen, he will take her by ship back to Greece and there put her to death.

Hecuba at this point moves out of the passive role that she has played so far, accepting the blows of misfortune. She begs Menelaus to kill Helen here in Troy, and persuades him to allow a debate in which Hecuba herself will be prosecutor. Helen speaks first, her defence like the preceding choral ode brings together the important themes of marriage and responsibility for the war; however she does not confine herself to accusing Trojans for what has happened. She blames Hecuba for giving birth to Paris, Priam for not killing him once he was born; she goes on to blame the three goddesses who made Paris the judge of their beauty, especially Aphrodite who caused her to fall in love with Paris. Helen adds to the list of usual suspects, accusing Menelaus for leaving home while Paris was there, the Trojans who stopped her escaping once Paris was dead and Deiphobus who then forced her to become his wife. It is a common criticism of Helen in this scene that she appears foolish and shallow, her arguments specious and ridiculous. Maybe so, but her rhetoric is no less slippery than that of Hecuba when she comes to speak and it is in keeping with the information we are given in the rest of the play to consider everyone as in some way guilty of the total dissolution of the world of the city which the fall of Troy represents. Hecuba's response is disappointing, she loses some of her tragic dignity in her attack upon Helen, and her argumentation is no more convincing. Her speech also shows a confusion of values in her eagerness to condemn Helen; she says that Helen should have committed suicide when compelled to remain in Troy after Paris's death 'this is what a noble woman would have done' (1013-14), and yet she advises Andromache not to wish for death but accommodate herself to her new husband! Finally, in the name of the children of the Greeks (!) who have died, she pleads for Helen's execution. This episode of debate once more links Greeks and Trojans in the same pattern of guilt, indeed it is difficult to find sympathy for any of the speakers in the debate. Problems have arisen from the marriage of Helen and Menelaus but also from that of Hecuba and Priam who had been warned when she was pregnant with Paris that if allowed to survive he would destroy Troy. In a way the Greeks are only the mechanism of Troy's destruction which had been made inevitable by the flawed relations between Trojans and gods.

The last choral ode (1060-1117) recapitulates the fall of Troy and its implications. The gods seem not to care about honours paid to them by Trojans in the past, for now husbands lie unburied while wives and children are taken off into slavery and Helen still lives. Our sympathy is roused for Hecuba once more as she attends to the burial of Astyanax, although even in this she still clings to fabled Trojan pride. She mourns for the child who never had a share of the glory of Troy, a fine marriage, power and rule equal to that of the gods.

After Troy's future is wiped out with Astyanax, all that remains is to burn the city to the ground and remove the women to their new marriages. Hecuba attempts to rush into the flames, demonstrating as at the beginning of the play, her oneness with the city. The final dissolution describes Troy and Hecuba identically, collapsing to the ground.

Trojan Women may be episodic in construction but it is not unstructured. Every scene and choral ode is integrated and orchestrated towards this ending where we witness the complete dissolution of the city, and everything that it consists of: its wealth, walls, laws, religious rituals and family kinship groups. The causes of the disaster lie in Troy itself. Trojans have broken faith with the gods and with human conventions and relationships which the gods are thought to oversee. These include the sanctity of oaths, kingship, hospitality and family integrity. We are accustomed to see in Greek drama a view of marriage as the foundation of a prosperous city (*Eumenides* gives this notion its fullest expression). The other possibility presented here is that it can also be the ruin of the city. What makes the play satisfying as tragedy and appealing today is not just its harrowing look at the victims of war, but its moral ambiguity. Our sympathies are engaged for the suffering victims and we feel outrage at the brutality of the conquerors, but sadly the victims are not without blame.

Although we interpret the play for ourselves in the light of modern experience and behavioural standards we should not lose sight of its significance in its own time. This grim picture of a society destroyed by war with further disasters in prospect for the conquerors was presented by Euripides in 415 BC, when Athens had been at war for over fifteen years, but was still ten years away from final defeat. It is possible to read the play as directly related to contemporary situations, as a cautionary tale for Athenians, possibly a warning against arrogant, impious behaviour. However, such an interpretation is optimistic, it implies that things can get better, and there is no justification for this in *Trojan Women*. We see that the community or state is sick and that the sickness spreads down from the top, affecting even those parts that seem to function properly, the families of ordinary Trojan men and women. The theme of the disintegration of the city or public community, together with the related theme of the breakdown of marriage relationships continued to occupy

Euripides, as we can see from the two plays produced after his death when Athens was close to defeat.

In *Iphigeneia at Aulis* the demands of state destroy a family. Compelled by the people who are eager to go to war, Agamemnon decides to sacrifice his daughter, thus attacking his own family and giving Clytemnestra reasons to hate him. As in *Trojan Women*, all marriages mentioned in *Iphigeneia* are problematic and the depiction of the heroic leaders is anything but reassuring. However in *Bacchae*, produced in the same year (404 BC), we find the most complete and appalling picture of the disintegration of state and family alike. The disasters which befall the city of Thebes are also causally linked with men's behaviour towards the gods, and Dionysus as a character in the play coolly plans the details of destruction. *Trojan Women* therefore, like the words of Poseidon in the Prologue, warns us of worse things to come.

The Cassandra scene

Richard Rutherford

I shall discuss a single scene in the play and try to define its
dramatic and its distinctively Euripidean qualities. *Trojan
Women* begins with the majestic yet chilling encounter between
Poseidon and Athena, in which they make a compact to send
storms to scatter and reduce the returning Greek fleet. There-
after we move to the human level of action, and witness the
miserable laments of Hecuba and the women of Troy. Thus far
the play has been static, but the next sequence strikes a much
more rapid and agitated note.

The scene I shall consider is the one in which the prophetess
Cassandra enters in a state of wild excitement, exulting in her
'marriage' to Agamemnon, leader of the conquering army. The
Greek herald Talthybius, conversing with queen Hecuba, observes a burst of torch-flame from within the women's shelter. He
reacts with alarm, fearing the women indoors have decided to
burn themselves to death. Hecuba reassures him: 'There is no
fire. My daughter, Cassandra, in her madness is rushing out here
in a frenzy' (306-7). A moment later Cassandra enters bearing
torches, as though celebrating her own wedding. Her entrance-
song includes appeals to the god Hymenaeus, who presides over
marriage: in this first section she sings, in wild and emotional
metres. In the second part of the scene she calms down somewhat, enough to revert to normal spoken verse, and speaks more
lucidly to her mother. But her words are still allusive and hard
for the others to comprehend, as she foretells the misfortunes of
the Greeks on their journey home: the interminable wanderings
of Odysseus, and the humiliating end that awaits the triumphant
Agamemnon. It is a traditional feature of the legend that Cassandra's prophecies should not be believed, and neither the
sympathetic Hecuba nor the contemptuous Talthybius recognise
the truly ominous significance of her warnings. At the end of the
scene she is led away to the ships, bidding farewell to her mother
and her homeland, and anticipating her own death at Mycenae.

From entrance to exit she has dominated the stage for just over 150 lines; but she does not reappear in the play, and we are probably meant to suppose that her mother never sees her again. Cassandra, like other women in this play, is a victim of war and thus arouses our pity, but what other functions does this striking episode perform in the play?

The first point to make is one which looks back beyond Euripides to his great predecessor Aeschylus. The scene is in part a tribute to, and imitation of, the Cassandra scene in Aeschylus' Agamemnon, over four decades earlier. In that play, Agamemnon brings Cassandra home as a concubine, but she is a silent witness while Clytemnestra welcomes her husband home with hypocritical extravagance. Only after he has been lured inside does she break silence, and there too her utterances are first delivered in impassioned lyrics; only gradually does she shake off the burden of divine inspiration and speak more straightforwardly to the Chorus. There too she prophesies Agamemnon's death and her own; there too she renounces the trappings of Apollo; there too her predictions only confuse her audience, who do not understand or credit her words. What is different in Euripides is the tone of Cassandra's response to the situation; whereas in Aeschylus her mood is bitter yet resigned, in the new scene she is at first ecstatic in celebration of her 'wedding', then argues at length for the paradoxical conclusion that the Trojans are happier than the Greeks. The rhetorical ingenuity is typical of Euripides, and redolent of the age of the sophists; in the same way, Helen later argues that her abandonment of Menelaus was actually beneficial to Greece! Eccentric argumentation of this kind is not found in Aeschylus, and contributes to the more cerebral character of Euripidean tragedy. Emotional moments are handled in a complex though still moving way.

A second important point is that although this scene is the only one in which we, the modern audience, see Cassandra, we know that she appeared earlier in the trilogy. Euripides did not normally go in for connected trilogies, preferring to compose self-contained plays, but the Trojan trilogy of 415 was an exception. The first play, the *Alexandros*, concerned Paris' upbringing after being exposed as a child, and his reinstatement as a prince of Troy. The second, *Palamedes*, dealt with an episode on the Greek side during the course of the war. Neither survives, but we know a certain amount about them from indirect evidence. In particular, it seems clear that Cassandra spoke the prologue of the first play and that she described the danger that threatened Troy if Paris (Alexandros) was allowed to live: he would prove to be 'the ruin of Troy and the destruction of Pergamum'. However the plot of that play worked in detail, it is obvious that Cassandra's warnings were given in vain: Paris survived, was recognised and welcomed back as a favoured son, and proceeded to carry off Helen and bring retribution on Troy. Now, in the third play, Cassandra reappears and prophesies again. This time, the burden of her prediction is that the Greeks will pay dearly for their victory, and she presents this as cause for celebration and rejoicing among the Trojans. Her record so far makes the audience confident that this prophecy is true (it is confirmed not only by the tradition but also by the dialogue of Poseidon and Athena in this play); but this is cold comfort for the Trojans even if they did believe her – which they do not. The futility of Cassandra's prophetic gift is highlighted in both the *Alexandros* and the *Trojan Women*.

Thirdly, the dramatic technique of the scene needs some attention, and especially the formal aspects of song, speech and genre. The first part of the sequence, from Cassandra's entry at a run (307), involves wild and agitated song from the inspired maiden, who calls on Hymenaeus, Hecate and Apollo in a frenzied version of a marriage-song. At 342 the poet reverts to spoken verse (iambic trimeters, the normal metre for regular speech): the chorus-leader urges Hecuba to restrain Cassandra and prevent her from running off to the Greek camp, and Hecuba tries to recall her daughter to sanity. Cassandra's response is a long speech (353-405) in which she encourages her mother to rejoice, alludes to Agamemnon's death, and presents her arguments for the misery of the Greeks (they undertook a war for a bad woman, many of them died here, meanwhile their wives died childless back at home), and for the happiness of the Trojans (they died gloriously, fighting for their country; they were able to go home after the day's fighting, to their families; Hector was fortunate, because he, like the rest of the Trojans, gained undying fame from the war – which they could never have had if not for Paris' crime!).

The Chorus replies with a couplet of discontented bewilderment, referring to the obscurity of her words. Talthybius the herald is sterner: if she were not out of her mind, she would be punished for this sort of talk; and Agamemnon is a fool to fancy such a crazed woman (408ff.). This turns Cassandra's attention toward him: in another long speech she first denounces the sycophantic race of heralds, then reverts to foretelling misfortunes for the Greeks, including a catalogue of trials which will face Odysseus (424-43). Finally, her speech shifts from iambic trimeters to trochaic tetrameters, a longer line and a metre that Euripides seems regularly to use for scenes of fast movement, agitation or excitement; this is a signal that the emotional tempo and the frenzy of her inspiration – or her madness – are again on the increase. In this final section she reverts to the language of marriage, but with blacker and more macabre references to her own death and that of her 'bridegroom': 'let me marry my bridegroom in the house of Hades' (445); 'they will toss me out as a naked corpse, and the ravines will give me to wild beasts as their food, near my groom's grave ...' (448-9). In this section Cassandra's impatience is growing: bizarrely, she is eager to go aboard the ship which is to convey her into exile and slavery, unlike the rest of the women who dread the prospect of enslavement in foreign lands. She sees herself as an instrument of vengeance, a Fury; in conclusion, she declares that her forthcoming death will be an occasion for triumph: 'I will come victorious to the dead, after sacking the halls of the Atridae, by whom we were ruined' (460-1).

This description makes clear that the scene requires a virtuoso performance from the actor who plays Cassandra. The character swings between ecstatic inspiration and vigorous rationality; the mode of presentation alters in relation to this shift, from agitated singing to more measured but eloquent argument and up the scale again to emotional prophetic assertion. This kind of modulation between song and speech can be paralleled elsewhere in Greek tragedy: it figures in the scene in the *Agamemnon* which Euripides is imitating, and in other scenes involving passionate female characters in Euripides (the death of Alcestis in the play of that name; the delirium of Phaedra in *Hippolytus*, where the heroine eventually recovers her self-control and speaks more rationally). Here there is a generic aspect too: the earlier part of the scene is a kind of parody of a wedding song, as is shown not only by the invocations of Hymenaeus but by phrases such as 'blessed is the bridegroom' (311). Where a wedding-celebration should be a communal event, Cassandra here celebrates on her own, without support or justification: Agamemnon is not present, nor is the relationship which he contemplates with her one of marriage. Later indeed she speaks of the marriage as one which will be celebrated in Hades (see above). This kind of distortion of ritual, whereby something familiar and positive is transformed into a parodic or horrific form, is an extremely powerful and significant element in Greek tragedy: another example is the perversion of sacrificial ritual, as in the human sacrifice of figures such as Iphigeneia and Polyxena.

Just as the wedding-song is distorted and negated, so also is the formal rhetoric which Cassandra deploys in the second part of the scene. Rhetoric, as practised in the assembly and law-courts of Euripides' time, is normally regarded as the art of persuasion. At least ideally, it utilises reasoned arguments from evidence to reach generally acceptable conclusions with practical consequences. Here we see a kind of parodic rhetoric. First, the case which Cassandra is arguing is paradoxical, unbelievable, unacceptable to any of those present: neither the victorious Greeks nor the vanquished Trojans are going to agree that the Trojans are happier or better off than the Greeks. Secondly, in a normal rhetorical scenario it may be unlikely that an opponent will be convinced, but it is not impossible. In Cassandra's case, however, it is a fundamental feature of her mythic character, already familiar to Aeschylus' audience and certainly to Euripides', that her prophecies are not believed; so there is no chance of her convincing her audience of the truth of what she predicts. Thirdly, even if she did convince them, this can have no practical consequences. If Hecuba were, impossibly, to say 'Yes, you are right; the Trojans haven't had such a bad deal after all', it would make no difference to the sufferings in store. When characters in tragedy know the truth about the future, it rarely brings them much comfort: Oedipus' inadequate foresight is a case in point. Fourthly, although Cassandra's vision of the future is obviously true, for we know Agamemnon will die and the other Greeks will indeed suffer, her attitude to the whole situation remains peculiar, her reasoning skewed. Is this divine insight also a kind of delusion or insanity which leads her to see things in a false light? When Talthybius dismisses her as a mad-woman, he clearly does not look deep enough into what she says, but he is not altogether wrong either. The scene certainly leaves us unsure how to assess Cassandra, how far we should endorse her conviction that she will be the instrument of retribution for her people. Is this more than a grandiloquent piece of self-deception?

In both the sung and the spoken sections, then, we see a clearly deliberate distortion of generic conventions, which enhances our sense of the world of the play as a world in which all that is normal, comfortable or familiar to the women of Troy has been destroyed. Other parts of the play reinforce this perception: for example, the choral ode which follows the episode that includes the Cassandra scene, in which the women recall the ritual celebrations, song, music and public worship which followed the apparent departure of the Greek forces – celebrations which were then interrupted by the 'bloodthirsty shout' of warriors emerging from the horse (555-6).

It remains to say something about the place of the Cassandra scene in the structure of the *Trojan Women* as a whole. Although, as we have seen, there are connections on the level of plot with the rest of the trilogy (Cassandra prophesied evil to come in the first play, and now does so again), this still remains a strikingly self-contained and independent episode. Hecuba has barely reacted to the departure of Cassandra before further misfortunes ensue. Even in the speech she makes immediately after her daughter's exit, Cassandra's sorrows are only one topic among many: she is paired with Polyxena, and Hecuba as queen and royal mother sees herself as burdened by the catastrophe of all Troy. Some of the later scenes are dominated by Andromache and the fate of her son Astyanax, and by the confrontation of Hecuba with Helen; others are given up to lamentation and mourning for what is lost. This is not a tragedy which fits well with Aristotle's requirements that a drama should present an action, and that the plot should follow a necessary or probable sequence. There is no obvious reason arising from the plot for the Cassandra scene to come where it does, as opposed to later in the play, although there may be dramatic motivations for placing it early. The scene, that is, affects the audience emotionally, but has no consequences for the succeeding events of the play. Rather, the *Trojan Women* is made up of virtually self-contained episodes strung together, united by the continuous presence of the queen and the Chorus, individual and collective victims of the Greek victory.

To point this out is not to criticise the playwright. Aristotle also remarked, with rather patronising praise, that 'whatever other defects of organisation Euripides may have, he is the most intensely tragic of all the poets' – that is, the most skilled at arousing pity and fear, the quintessentially tragic emotions. Indeed, rather than assume that, living before Aristotle, he was not well-instructed enough in what a tragic plot ought to look like, it is better to allow that the dramatists could innovate, in structuring their plays as in the detail of the myths they used. If the *Trojan Women* lacks the 'necessary or probable sequence' of action, if it does not possess the forward impetus of *Oedipus* or *Medea*, that in itself may be expressive. Action by Hecuba, by Cassandra, by Andromache, by any of the women of Troy, is impossible. They are the victims; the trophies of war are passive. This is not a play about heroic action or initiative or self-sacrifice. At most it is a play of suffering, which is indeed intense and prolonged but which it would be strange to call heroic. As in other places (for instance, *Heracles*), Euripides uses structure to convey meaning – to express through a series of exceptionally bleak and uncompromising episodes the unalloyed horror that follows on total defeat in war. Whether we focus on Cassandra's delusion or Hecuba's despair, *Trojan Women* is a tragedy as dark as any in the Greek canon.

Because the continuum of myth extends beyond the fate of a single individual or family or even a single city, every Greek tragedy ends with something else still in store. In some tragedies closure is imposed more firmly than in others, but in many the events still in store are of great importance in shaping our attitude to the whole play. In Euripides' *Medea*, the Athenian audience would have been aware that Medea would not only find refuge in Athens (as foreseen with dismay by the Chorus of that play) but would gain an ascendancy over gullible king Aegeus and eventually threaten the life of the Athenians' favourite hero Theseus. At the conclusion of Sophocles' *Oedipus at Colonos*, Antigone departs for Thebes, determined to bury her brother Polynices; the whole plot of the *Antigone* is foreshadowed, making very clear that the passing of old Oedipus does not bring the action to a final or satisfying close.

What of the aftermath of *Trojan Women*? It is obvious that Euripides intends to keep the subsequent events very much in our minds: the dialogue between Athena and Poseidon predicts the dispersal of the Greek fleet; the Trojan women anxiously wonder who their masters will be, and where they will each be taken; the prophecies of Cassandra foretell the fate of Agamemnon and Odysseus, as well as hinting at the transformation of her mother into animal form; the Helen-scene anticipates the renewed infatuation of Menelaus with his guileful and beguiling wife. In a way, then, the Trojan sufferings are balanced by the future sufferings of the Greeks; but it is obvious that this does not cancel out the present agonies of those who have lost their city, or of Andromache who has lost her husband and within the play has to lose her son to a particularly brutal and barbaric death. According to Cassandra, she is the victor, and the Trojans are happier than the Greeks. This conviction, though it may be divinely inspired, is denied by any human audience of the play. Euripides seems to have included the Cassandra scene in part to show how futile such calculations of future compensation must be when the present suffering is real and undeniable and immediate. 'Look to the end' is traditional Greek wisdom, and comes naturally to one who is detached, an onlooker or adviser (like Solon in Herodotus). When it comes from one who is herself involved in calamity, it can only bring consolation because she is mad.

Discussion of the conclusions of plays and tales provides a suitable point of closure, and it is time that this essay reached its end.

Appendix
aod productions

1993
February   *Hekabe*
August-October   *Hekabe & Hippolytus*

1994
February-March   *Electra*
September-November *Antigone*

1995
September-November *Oedipus the King*
September   *Blow your mind, Aristophanes!*

1996
February-March   *Trojan Women*
September-November *Medea*

1997
February-March   *Electra*
June   *Matricide without tears*, broadcast on BBC
                      Radio 3
August   *Medea*, release of audiobook by Penguin Books
September-November *Ajax*
October   *The face of tragedy*, release of video

1998
February-March   *Antigone*
September-November *Oedipus the King*

1999
February-March   *Hippolytus*
September-November *Agamemnon*

2000
January-April   *Grave gifts*
September-December *Bacchae*

aod productions

2001
January-April   *Medea*
September-December   *Antigone*

2002
January-May   *Trojan Women*
September-December   *Electra*

2003
January-April   *Agamemnon*
April-May   *Bacchae* & *Grave gifts* (performances in
                             ancient theatres of Ephesus and Aspendus)
September-December   *Oedipus the King*

2004
January-March   *Trojan Women* & *Hippolytus*

2005
September-December   *Trojan Women*

2006
September-December   *Oedipus*

2007
May-November   *Bacchic*

2008
February-June   *Bacchic*

actors of dionysus

14 Cuthbert Road
Brighton BN2 0EN
tel/fax 01273 692 604
www.actorsofdionysus.com

136

Suggestions for further reading

The talks in this volume are selected from *Dionysus*, the journal of **aod**, and from:

Shasha, T. & Stuttard, D., *Essays on Bacchae* (**aod**, 2006).
Stuttard, D. & Shasha, T., *Essays on Trojan Women* (**aod**, 2001).

Greek tragedy in general

Brown, A.L., *A New Companion to Greek Tragedy* (Croom Helm, 1983): a dictionary of Greek tragedy.
Csapo, E. & Slater, W.J., *The Context of Ancient Drama* (University of Michigan Press, 1995): a sourcebook.
Lowe, N.J., *The Classical Plot and the Invention of Western Narrative* [especially chapter 8] (Cambridge University Press, 2000).

The following two companions have contributions from a number of scholars and offer an introduction to the range of contemporary interest in tragedy:

Easterling, P. (ed.), *The Cambridge Companion to Greek Tragedy* (Cambridge University Press, 1997).
Gregory, J. (ed.), *A Companion to Greek Tragedy* (Blackwell, 2005).

These two volumes represent different approaches and have both been highly influential:

Goldhill, S., *Reading Greek Tragedy* (Cambridge University Press, 1986).
Taplin, O., *Greek Tragedy in Action* (Methuen, 1978).

Euripides

Morwood, J., *The Plays of Euripides* (Bristol Classical Press, 2002).
Barlow, S.A., *The Imagery of Euripides*, 3rd edn (Bristol Classical Press, 2008).
Halleran, M., *Stagecraft in Euripides* (Croom Helm, 1985).

Suggestions for further reading

Individual plays

Three series are represented here. That of Cambridge University Press has new translations with brief facing commentary and short introductions. The Aris & Phillips series has introduction, Greek text with facing translation, and detailed commentary keyed to the translation. The Duckworth series is designed to offer accessible introductions. More detailed bibliographies can be found in the Duckworth and Aris & Phillips volumes.

Franklin, D., *Euripides: Bacchae* (Cambridge University Press, 2000).

Mills, S., *Euripides: Bacchae*, Duckworth Companions to Greek and Roman Tragedy (Duckworth, 2006).

Seaford, R., *Euripides: Bacchae*, with Introduction, Translation and Commentary (Aris & Phillips, 1996, 2001).

Allan, W., *Euripides: Medea*, Duckworth Companions to Greek and Roman Tragedy (Duckworth, 2002).

Harrison, J., *Euripides: Medea*, translated with commentary (Cambridge University Press, 2000).

Page, D.L., *Euripides: Medea* (Oxford University Press, 1938).

Halleran, M.R., *Euripides: Hippolytus*, with Introduction, Translation and Commentary (Aris & Phillips, 1995, 2000).

Mills, S., *Euripides: Hippolytus*, Duckworth Companions to Greek and Roman Tragedy (Duckworth, 2002).

Shaw, B., *Euripides: Hippolytus* (Cambridge University Press, 2007).

Cropp, M.J., *Euripides: Electra*, with Introduction, Translation and Commentary (Aris & Phillips, 1988).

Barlow, S., *Euripides: Trojan Women*, with Introduction, Translation and Commentary (Aris & Phillips, 1986).

Goff, B., *Euripides: Trojan Women*, Duckworth Companions to Greek and Roman Tragedy (Duckworth, forthcoming).

Stuttard, D., *Introduction to Trojan Women*, including an adaptation of the play (Company Dionysus, 2005).

Translations

All the translations and adaptations by David Stuttard which were used in **aod** productions are available from Company Dionysus. Other translations are available in Penguin or Oxford World's Classics series.

Suggestions for further reading

Audiobooks

Actors of Dionysus (**aod**), *Euripides: Medea* (Penguin, 1997).
Stuttard, D., *Trojan Women,* after Euripides (Company Dionysus, 2005).

DVDs

Actors of Dionysus, *Bacchic* (**aod**, 2007).
Actors of Dionysus, *The Face of Tragedy* (**aod**, 1997).

ALSO AVAILABLE

Classical World Series

GREEK TRAGEDY:
AN INTRODUCTION
Marion Baldock

ISBN 978 1 85399 119 6

In this useful Introduction to the subject, Marion Baldock traces the development and performance of Greek tragedy with detailed chapters on each of the three main tragic poets: Aeschylus, Sophocles and Euripides. Specific plays and topics are covered, and one chapter compares the different treatments of the 'Electra' theme by each dramatist.

With illustrations, quotations from the plays in English, an annotated bibliography and suggestions for further study, this is an invaluable guide to the tragic genre.

Marion Baldock (now Gibbs) is head of James Allen's Girls' School, London.

Titles in the Classical World series are designed for students and teachers of ancient history and classical civilisation at late school and early university levels.

Classical World Series

THE PLAYS OF
EURIPIDES
James Morwood

ISBN 978 1 85399 614 6

No book in English covering all the plays of Euripides has been published since 1967. In the meantime there has been something of a revolution in the way we view classical drama generally and Euripides in particular. *The Plays of Euripides* reflects that revolution and aims to show how Euripides was continually reinventing himself. A truly Protean figure, he seems to set out on a new journey in each of his surviving nineteen plays.

Between general introduction and final summary, Morwood's chapters identify the themes that underlie the plays and concentrate, above all, on demonstrating the extraordinary diversity of this great dramatist.

James Morwood is Emeritus Fellow of Wadham College, Oxford, and the author of many books, including, as translator, *Euripides: Medea and Other Plays* (Oxford World's Classics, 1998) and *Euripides: The Trojan Women and Other Plays* (Oxford World's Classics, 2001).

Companions to Greek and Roman Tragedy

EURIPIDES: BACCHAE
Sophie Mills

ISBN 978 0 7156 3430 1

References to Dionysus in popular culture focus on the god as the incarnation of wild and decadent behaviour, by which humans are intrigued and appalled. The god as he is portrayed in Euripides' *Bacchae* is, however, more complex, paradoxically transcending straightforward notions of the Dionysiac. Euripides' Dionysus blurs the dividing line between many of the fundamental categories of ancient Greek life — male and female, Greek and barbarian, divine and human. This book explores his place in Athenian religion, what Euripides makes of him in the play, and the views of later writers and scholars.

Sophie Mills is Associate Professor and Chair of Classics, University of North Carolina at Asheville. She is the author of *Theseus, Tragedy and the Athenian Empire* (Oxford University Press, 1997) and of a volume on the *Hippolytus* in this series.

Titles in the Companions to Greek and Roman Tragedy series are accessible introductions to ancient tragedies. Each volume discusses the main themes of a play and the central developments in modern criticism, while also addressing the play's historical context and the history of its performance and adaptation.

Companions to Greek and Roman Tragedy

EURIPIDES: MEDEA
William Allen

ISBN 978 0 7156 3187 4

Euripides' *Medea* is one of the greatest and most influential Greek tragedies. This companion to the play outlines the development of the Medea myth before Euripides and explores his uniquely powerful version from various angles. There are chapters on the play's relationship to the gender politics of fifth-century Athens, Medea's status as a barbarian, and the complex moral and emotional impact of her revenge. Particular attention is paid to the tragic effect of Medea's great monologue and the significance of her role as a divine avenger. The book ends by considering the varied and fascinating reception of Euripides' play from antiquity to the present day.

William Allan is Tutor and Fellow of University College Oxford, and the author of *The Andromache and Euripidean Tragedy* (Oxford University Press, 2000) and *Euripides: The Children of Heracles* (Aris and Phillips, 2001).

Companions to Greek and Roman Tragedy

EURIPIDES: HIPPOLYTUS
Sophie Mills

ISBN 978 0 7156 2974 1

The *Hippolytus* is generally acknowledged to be one of Euripides' finest tragedies, for the construction of its plot, its use of language and its memorable characterisations of Phaedra and Hippolytus. Furthermore, it asks serious and disturbing questions about the influence of divinity on human lives. Sophie Mills considers these and many other themes in detail, setting the play in its mythological, cultural and historical contexts. She also includes discussions of major trends in interpretations of the play and of subsequent adaptations of the *Hippolytus* story, from Seneca to Mary Renault and beyond.

Sophie Mills is Associate Professor and Chair of Classics, University of North Carolina at Asheville. She is the author of *Theseus, Tragedy and the Athenian Empire* (Oxford University Press, 1997) and of a volume on the *Bacchae* in this series.

Companions to Greek and Roman Tragedy

EURIPIDES: TROJAN WOMEN
Barbara Goff

ISBN 978 0 7156 3545 2

Euripides' *Trojan Women* is a devastating play, acclaimed throughout the twentieth century as one of theatre's most powerful anti-war statements. Set at the end of the Trojan war, it depicts the women of Troy as they wait for the departure of the Greek ships that will take them into slavery. Barbara Goff sets the play in its historical, dramatic and literary contexts, and provides a scene-by-scene analysis which brings out the pace and intellectual vigour of the play. The main themes are fully discussed, such as the relations between men and women, Greeks and barbarians, and divine and human, the identity of victory and defeat, and the power of theatre. The final chapter, which deals with the reception of the play, offers new insights into several modern works.

Barbara Goff is Professor of Classics, University of Reading. She is the author of *The Noose of Words* (1990) and *Citizen Bacchae: women's ritual practice in ancient Greece* (2004), and co-author with Michael Simpson of *Crossroads in the Black Aegean: Oedipus, Antigone and Dramas of the African Diaspora* (2007).